D1633967

THE DICED CAP

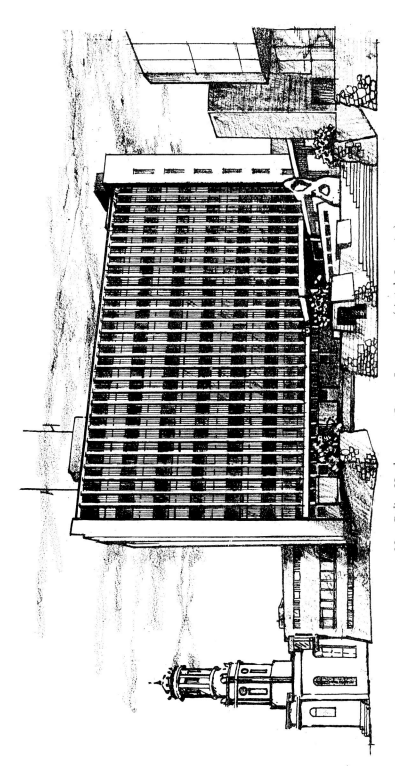

New Police Headquarters, Queen Street, 1972 (*Artist's Impression*)

THE
DICED CAP

THE STORY OF ABERDEEN CITY POLICE

with an Introduction by
FENTON WYNESS
K.ST.J, F.R.I.B.A, D.A

published by
THE CHIEF CONSTABLE
on behalf of
the Corporation of the City of
ABERDEEN

First Published 1972
©
Corporation of the City of Aberdeen

Printed in Great Britain at
The University Press
Aberdeen

13929

Contents

CHAPTERS   Page

APPENDICES

LINE DRAWINGS

PLATES

Preface

The Diced Cap is about Aberdeen and those men and women who have helped to police it from the twelfth century to the present day. Most of the information has come from Town Council Minutes, police records and from the various journals and publications of the times.

In preparing this account, Inspector Hamish Irvine has been indebted to many people: to Mr Fenton Wyness the well-known Aberdeen historian and writer, who not only wrote the introduction, but also gave much helpful advice and guidance; to Mr George Mackie of Gray's School of Art and Mr Ian Cargill of Aberdeen University Television Department for their professional services; to Mr Colin McLaren, Aberdeen University Archivist and Keeper of Manuscripts for the transcription of the Orders and Instructions to Constables in 1657; to Miss Margaret P. Rust, City Archivist and the staff of the local history department of Aberdeen Public Library for their kind co-operation; to Mr Wilson Smith one-time Burgh Prosecutor for his professional advice; and finally to Aberdeen Town Council for their willingness to finance the publication.

On behalf of Aberdeen City Police, may I say thank you to all these people for their generous assistance.

The Diced Cap shows how, in early days, the Police Force grew in response to a demand on the part of the public, who felt that an organised body was needed to fight widespread crime and protect life and property. To begin with it developed slowly, sometimes painfully, but the working conditions of the men, more often than not, reflected the conditions of ordinary people at the time. Our story is therefore in many ways, your story.

The book tells not only how Aberdeen's Police Force has developed, but also recalls many of the outstanding trials, cases and events over the years; including the famous trial of Jeannie Donald, the notorious Nellfield Cemetery Scandals and the tragic Torry Ferryboat disaster.

Aberdeen City Police is on the threshold of a new era. The old Lodge Walk Headquarters will soon be part of history, for the Force is about to remove to a modern headquarters in Queen Street, and if the proposed reorganisation of local government takes effect, the Force may soon form part of the police serving the north-east region, thus ending its independent status.

The public demand which called for the formation of a police force in this city so many years ago was motivated by a desire to prevent further deterioration in law and order at that time. The same is equally true today and an efficient police force which carries out its duties with integrity and courtesy can enrich the quality of life in any society.

The Force has served the community of Aberdeen well and contributed much to the efficiency of the police service generally. *The Diced Cap* records many of these achievements and much more. It is the life story of Aberdeen City Police.

Chief Constable

Introduction
by
Fenton Wyness

When any organisation functions quietly, smoothly and efficiently, the service it renders to the community is generally taken for granted. Such a body is the Aberdeen City Police. Of course the uniformed members of the Force are a familiar part of city life, yet they represent only a fraction of a vast, intricate and highly specialised structure of law enforcement about which the public knows little or nothing.

Although crime is as old as mankind, civilization is always progressing. However, there is little indication that law-breaking and vice are likely to be eliminated or even diminish in the foreseeable future — indeed the reverse seems possible. Progress not only brings benefits, it also initiates fresh opportunities for crime and licentiousness. Of necessity, therefore, the Police must ever keep one step ahead.

It is generally accepted that the judicial system in Scotland was introduced by King David I (1124–1153). Feudal in conception, it naturally met with strong opposition from the descendants of the ancient Celtic dynasties but eventually compromise was reached and by the end of his reign, David I had succeeded in uniting the whole of Scotland under his personal rule.

Initially, David's judicial system was very similar to that of England — not surprising when one recalls that, as an English landowner, he had lived there for many years. Among the changes he made was the appointment of Justiciaries — originally hereditary officers — to administer his laws against treason, crimes of violence and other major issues. He also created Royal burghs and burghs of barony vested with the necessary powers to maintain his laws in their own areas. These policies were continued by David's immediate successors and so it is said 'Scotland became a law-abiding country, except in the remote Highlands'.

The City of Aberdeen was one of those early Royal burghs created by David I. Such creation appears to have been initially a declaratory one but its establishment was confirmed as a charter granted *circa* 1179 by his grandson William the Lion (1165–1214). Among all the Scottish

Royal burghs, Aberdeen holds a unique place in that its municipal records are the most complete. Commencing in the year 1398 — with a fragment for the year 1317 — they cover the city's story for a period of over five hundred years. Unfortunately, one volume (1414–1433) is missing; it is believed to have been sent to Edinburgh as evidence in some legal dispute and was never returned. From these remarkable records much interesting information may be extracted.

In the early days of David's judicial system it would seem that, broadly speaking, crimes of violence were dealt with by the Crown while vice and licentiousness were concerns of the Church. Under the system, Royal burghs were bound by the king's *Leges Burgorum* — burgh laws — whereby the provost and baillies were responsible for keeping law and order within their burgh's boundaries.

In Aberdeen, three 'Heid Courtis' were held annually — the Michaelmas sitting being mainly devoted to the election of the provost and baillies for the ensuing year. When elected, they were required to take an oath of allegiance to the king and to the maintenance of his laws. The provost and baillies dealt with routine law-breaking while serious crimes were remitted to the visiting Justiciary. On rare occasions, such as when on a Royal progress, the king himself presided at 'Heid Courtis'. Eventually, the proceedings at these Courts were recorded and it is interesting to note that the city's Baillie Court Books begin in the year 1572. Burghs of barony — such as Old Aberdeen — functioned in a similar manner, the Bishop of Aberdeen presiding in his capacity as baron of the barony.

Regarding legal procedure in those far-off days, one can only hazard a guess that basically it took the form of what eventually became known as Scots law. Naturally, Scots law differs from English law — indeed many authorities hold that the former is the better system. Having its roots deep in the remote Celtic past, Scots law is said to have evolved during the Middle Ages when Scotland, engaged in her lengthy wars with England, became more closely drawn to France and the continent than to her near neighbour. It is suggested that many principles of Roman law were then incorporated in the legal system and remained; indeed it has been said of the future — should Great Britain enter the Common Market, Scottish lawyers will feel more at home in dealing with cases than will their English brethren! Nowadays, of course, there is a tendency for Scots and English law to come into alignment as so much Parliamentary legislation affects both countries.

By present-day standards, punishments for crime in bygone days seem unusually severe. Decapitation, hanging and burning were commonplace for human life was then held very cheaply and there is little doubt the gibbets were seldom empty — perhaps as a warning to others! Until 1747, when feudal jurisdiction was abolished in Scotland, the grisly remains of criminals hanging from wayside gallows was a common sight. The last burning took place in Aberdeen in 1740 and the last public hanging in 1857. The municipal office of hangman was abolished in 1834.

Naturally enough, with little in the way of excitement or entertainment in their daily lives, a public execution was a most popular event, especially with women. Executions were largely attended by the citizens as contemporary accounts succinctly tell — '*Burning of Thomas Leyis: spars to withstand the press of the pepill: two broken — 8/8d.*' Aberdeen's *Black Kalendar* re-issued in 1845, gives detailed accounts of many of these public executions.

Up to the time of the Reformation, little appears to have been recorded about vice and licentiousness in the city — the concern of the Church. From this, one must not assume the Aberdonians were paragons of virtue until the advent of John Knox! The most likely explanation is that such records as may have existed were destroyed in 1559 when the churches and religious houses were pillaged and wrecked by 'Knox's Rabble'. However, subsequent to the Reformation, there is ample evidence of the citizens' wickedness, the variety of crimes committed, and the punishments meted out.

For example, in 1562, an unfortunate but spirited young lady wearing men's clothing '*passing the bounds of modestie*' and dancing in '*ane wanton and unchaste form in the companie of men*' was condemned to the stool of repentance in St Nicholas Kirk, while in 1640, a woman of doubtful morals had her head shaved and was chained to the Market Cross. She too ended on the stool of repentance. The 'Holy Willies' and 'Unco Gweed' of the reformed church were certainly zealous, especially in their endeavours to uphold the local dignitaries and several cases are recorded of citizens whose 'crimes' consisted merely of giving the provost and baillies a piece of their mind! Having been substantially fined, these unfortunates also finished up on the stool of repentance upholding the dignity of the occasion by appearing in sackcloth with ashes strewn in their hair! Absence from '*Sermon*', from '*Catechism*', and '*drinking on the Sabbath*', were other common 'crimes' — particularly the latter for in those days public houses never closed! Licensing hours were not introduced until 1854. In 1753 an unusual 'crime' — at least in those days — was committed — the publishing of a rash statement in the local Press. The writer of the statement was severely admonished; the editor was obliged to apologise — but the offending newspaper, the *Aberdeen Journal*, was condemned to be publicly burned in the Castlegate by the common hangman!

Although from early times, the responsibility for 'keeping the King's peace' in the burgh was a civic duty, there does not appear to have been any form of law enforcement before the middle of the sixteenth century when 'toun's guards' are first mentioned. These 'guards' were actually the Town Sergeants whose activities included many duties later undertaken by the police. They also acted as a day-time patrol throughout the burgh.

Following the Union of the Crowns in 1603, an Act of Parliament was passed with the idea of establishing Justices of the Peace in Scotland to administer the law and to appoint regular constables. This Act of 1617 failed to achieve its objectives but in Aberdeen there developed from it in 1638 a system of part-time constables drawn from the citizens to 'police' the four Quarters of the burgh. These Quarters were the predecessors of the Municipal Wards.

In 1655, during the Commonwealth, another attempt was made to establish Justices of the Peace in Scotland. It also failed and on the Restoration of King Charles II (1660–1685), the provisions made in 1617 were re-enacted. Thus feudal jurisdiction remained while the possibility of an organised constabulary moved further away.

Aberdeen's first regular 'police' were established in the year 1816 — 'The Night-Watch' which anticipated the Police Act of 1818 and in consequence was already an active body when the Act came into force. From this 'Night-Watch', Aberdeen's City Police originated.

Over the years, the evolution of the City Police has been gradual — until the last four decades when development has been rapid and spectacular, as witnessed by the impressive new Headquarters now rising on the site so long associated with police activity. At the outset, attempts at organisation were fumbling and haphazard — parochial efforts, hampered chiefly by the Aberdonian's inborn 'grippiness'; occasionally by a genuine lack of the necessary 'bawbees'; and not infrequently by pettiness on the part of the governing bodies involved. Sometimes one is left wondering how the Force ever survived its initial difficulties — but it did — yet, even when financial assistance was forthcoming, the dismal short-sightedness of the Magistrates all but wrecked the growing organisation.

The Diced Cap tells the story of the Force's vicissitudes and its progression from small beginnings as an independent local body. It discloses many interesting facts in cases the Force has been called upon to solve, among them crimes of violence, theft, fire-raising and fraud — and it reveals something of the dexterity with which the controlling authorities 'passed the buck' when occasion demanded! *The Diced Cap* also points the way to the future as outlined in *The Wheatley Report.*

45 Salisbury Terrace
Aberdeen

Chapter One

1124-1818

'You shall apprehend all suspicious persons who are night walkers, all vagabonds, all idle sturdy beggars and Egyptians (gypsies), all idle persons who have no means to live upon and will not betake themselves to some trade and all guilty of slaughter, murder or theft. You shall report for prosecution all Sabbath-breakers, all who are found taking the name of God in vain, all who are found swearing or cursing especially in the open streets, all fornicators and whoremongers, all drunkards such as haunt taverns after nine o'clock at night and all children come to the years of discretion that are disobedient to parents.'

These instructions to Aberdeen's part-time constables are from the Justice Court Book of 1657, but long before then there is evidence of law enforcement and justice in North-East Scotland; a justice which, in some respects, was as hard as its native granite.

Most writers agree that the history of Aberdeen as a Royal burgh goes back to the twelfth century, to the reign of King David I. No Charter from David I exists — indeed it may only have been a verbal promise made by the king to the citizens — but confirmation of the agreement then made is given in a Charter granted to the town about 1179 by King David's grandson, King William the Lion.

David's action in raising Aberdeen to the dignity of a Royal burgh stimulated its growth as a self-governing community and led to the emergence of an influential merchant class, the Burgesses of Guild or of Trade.

David also inaugurated laws known as *Leges Burgorum* or Burgh Laws, which provided *inter alia* that every Royal burgh in Scotland should hold annually three 'Heid Courtis' at which burgesses would hold council. Failure of burgesses to attend carried a sanction: 'gif onie burgiss beis absent therefra, not having ane lauchful essoszie, sic as be reasonn of sickness, by neuly getting ane wife, or beis at mercate or faire, he sall pay IV pennies.' It was at the Michaelmas Head Court in subsequent years that the Provost and Baillies were elected and it was a duty of the newly-elected Provost to select twelve of the wisest burgesses to take the oath 'to guard and maintain the burgh's laws and customs'. How the Provost assessed the wisdom of his fellow burgesses is not recorded!

It was King David too who created the office of Justiciar, the judge who travelled the country administering the 'King's Peace'. In Aberdeen the Justiciar had his own residence on the east side of Castle Street, and the court was held in the open air on the Heading Hill.

Castle Street has been the city centre and, indeed, the focal point of justice for upwards of six hundred years as the various names suggest: Justice Street, the Heading Hill, the Gallow Hill, Hangman's Brae and Correction Wynd. (Appendix I.)

By a Charter granted by Robert III on 20 October 1394, the building of a Tolbooth and Court House was sanctioned in the Castlegate. It comprised what was known as the 'Laigh Tolbooth' and the 'High Tolbooth', the former being the Council Chamber and Court House, the latter the city's first prison. This prison was known as 'Mids o' Mar' on the same sardonic principle by which the famous Edinburgh jail was called 'The Heart of Midlothian'.

Castle Street has the doubtful distinction of having been the last of several places of public execution in the city. It was last used for this purpose in 1857 when John Booth was hanged for murdering his mother-in-law at Oldmeldrum. The site of the original 'Hanging Stane' is marked by a small rectangular stone set in the carriageway near the entrance of Lodge Walk and opposite the top of Marischal Street; hence the expression 'I'll see you looking down Marischal Street' was but a euphemism for, 'I'll see you hanged'.

Justice Street derived its name from The Justice Port or 'Thief's Port'. First mentioned in 1440, it stood at the north-east corner of Castlegate and remained there till 1759 when it was demolished. This interesting Port derived its name from the practice of leading criminals through it to the places of execution, either the Heading Hill or the Gallow Hill. It was also the custom to display over the Port the heads or dismembered limbs of noted criminals.

From the foregoing we learn something of the existence in early times of a somewhat harsh system of executing justice, at least by present-day standards. Officials responsible for enforcing the law did not appear until the middle of the sixteenth century. These officials were the Town Sergeants, who were then called the 'Toun's Guards'. The earliest records of their activities show that they undertook duties now devolving on the Police Force. They were full-time employees and were the Magistrates' Officers in the civil and criminal courts.

Their duties included searching for and apprehending offenders; citing witnesses; attending precognitions and searching for stolen property. They also acted as a 'Day Patrole' in the burgh, taking their instructions from the Town Clerk and Procurator-Fiscal. At the outset their remuneration was small and a Council minute of 1563 shows they were entitled to receive annually fees of four shillings from every burgess and two shillings from every craftsman. It would seem they were not provided with uniform until 1615 when the five Town Sergeants were authorised to be clothed in a 'juip of reid staymn (tunic of red worsted cloth) haveing the toun's armis embroyderit thereon'. Their role as police officers continued as late as 1865 as shown in their Rules and Regulations for that year. (Appendix II.)

In 1617, fourteen years after the Union of the Crowns, King James VI's government passed an Act of Parliament designed to establish Justices of the Peace in Scotland to administer the law and with power to appoint constables who, it was hoped, would 'detect and pursue offenders, arrest and bring before the Justices all vagabonds, sturdy beggars and Egyptians, and suspect persons who sleepeth all the day and walketh in the night'.

However, this Act of 1617 failed to achieve its objective, largely because it safeguarded the existing principle of hereditary jurisdiction. Consequently, many barons of barony continued to enjoy the privileges of hereditary jurisdiction and held their own barony courts, thus rendering the parliamentary scheme unworkable.

Despite the failure of this legislation there developed from it the practice of nominating citizens drawn from all walks of life to be constables for a year, on a part-time basis. In October 1638, the burgh records minute for the first time an election of constables to the four Quarters of the town: Fittie, the Green, the Crooked and Even. These four Quarters were the predecessors of the present-day Municipal Wards instituted in 1833. A Town Sergeant, known as a 'Quarter Officer', was appointed to each Quarter and under his direction and control the part-time constables operated.

In November 1655, during the Commonwealth period, another attempt was made to establish Justices of the Peace and Constables in Scotland. The latter were to have the same responsibilities as detailed in the Act of 1617, with the additional responsibility of enforcing a Statute 'for the better observance of the Lord's Day'. They were to have powers to enter any house where the inmates were suspected of 'profaning the Sabbath'. As one might expect, the Ordinance of 1655 failed. The duties contained in the 1617 Act were accordingly undertaken by the part-time constables and the first orders to these appear in the Aberdeen Justice Court Book for 1657. (Appendix III.)

Following the Commonwealth came the Restoration of the Monarchy and in 1661 King Charles II re-enacted the provisions made in 1617, but as he re-established hereditary jurisdiction, the idea of an organised constabulary was again dropped. However, the need for an effective system of policing became increasingly apparent during the eighteenth century. Serious crime was on the increase while rioting and kidnapping were commonplace.

Kidnapping was particularly prevalent from 1740 to 1746 and the port of Aberdeen figured prominently in it. Men and women, boys and girls — some only six years old — were abducted and transported as slaves to the American plantations. Many well known people were involved, among them Baillie William Fordyce and the Town Clerk Depute Walter Cochran. Every ruse imaginable, including bribery, false promises, intoxicants, threats and even violence, was employed to procure victims for this slave trade. The shameful practice was obviously carried out quite openly, a house in the Green and even the Tolbooth being used as places of confinement for victims awaiting transportation by slave-ship. More than six hundred people were believed to have been abducted from the Aberdeen area alone and sold into slavery for periods of five years and more. Widespread misery was caused by this despicable trading in human lives but the influential positions held by some of the organisers appears to have rendered them immune from criminal prosecution. It is known that the father of one boy who had been kidnapped did endeavour to seek redress by civil action but none of the law officers of the time could be prevailed upon to execute the summons against those thought to be responsible.

It was not until 1758 that the villainy of the kidnappers came into the open, when a young man Peter Williamson, who had been abducted as a child in Aberdeen and sold as a slave in Pennsylvania, returned to the city. In a pamphlet he exposed the kidnapping system. The Magistrates immediately accused him of 'a scurrilous and infamous libel on the Corporation of the City of Aberdeen and the whole members thereof'. He was charged by them, convicted and imprisoned until he signed a retraction. He was then fined and banished from the town. However, Williamson was made of sterner stuff. In 1762, he brought a civil action against the Corporation and won his case. He was awarded one hundred pounds damages and eighty pounds costs. Six years later he took similar action against Baillie Fordyce and others, and again won his case, obtaining two hundred pounds damages and one hundred guineas costs — quite a considerable sum of money in those days. The kidnapping scandal must have occasioned much public comment at the time and the need for an effective body to secure justice must have been apparent to all. Yet it was not until fifteen years later, 24 April 1783, that the Aberdeen Magistrates appointed Mr Charles Clapperton to the post of 'Town Keeper and whole-time Constable'. His duties (Appendix IV) justify his being regarded as the city's first professional constable and, although his powers were limited, his appointment was a progressive step.

An even more important step was taken in 1795, when the Aberdeen Police Act vested executive power in thirteen citizens — Commissioners of Police — selected by the inhabitants to provide for 'better paving, lighting, cleansing and other improvements'. Unfortunately, their efforts were badly handicapped by the lack of a law enforcement body under their control.

The need for an effective Police Force again became apparent in a most distressing event which took place in Castle Street during the evening of 4 June 1802. A contemporary report describes how on that date a detachment of the Ross and Cromarty Rangers, then stationed at Castlehill Barracks, mingled with the crowd in Castle Street, after formal celebrations in honour of King George III's birthday. It appears that about half past seven in the evening some of the officers, who had been at a banquet and were somewhat intoxicated, came in for some leg-pulling by a party of roughnecks. Resenting this attack on their dignity, the officers ordered the soldiers to load their muskets.

Provost James Hadden, who had been dining with the officers, was hastily called to the scene. He read the 'Riot Act' and the situation quietened down, the soldiers being ordered back to Barracks. Unfortunately, as they marched off, further abuse was hurled at them. The officers ordered them to about-turn and fire into the crowd. Four people were killed and ten or twelve injured. With a view to avoiding dire consequences, the regiment wisely left town during the night.

Two officers and two sergeants were subsequently indicted and tried in Edinburgh for wilful murder. They were acquitted. A disturbing feature of the case was that the Lord Advocate refused to institute proceedings and it was left to Daniel Ross, a wood sawyer, to prosecute for the death of his son, an on-looker, who had been shot in the head. It was long before the days of legal assistance. Ross's case was financed by public subscription.

In 1816 Thomas Burnett, one of the Police Commissioners, was appointed convener of a committee formed to 'consider the most prompt and effectual means of establishing a nightly watch for the general protection of the property of the inhabitants against the attempts of some daring depredators who have recently attempted to enter the habitations of the citizens in almost every quarter of the town and on different occasions have plundered the places where they have actually entered of whatever was within their reach.'

As a result of Burnett's report it was agreed to establish a Night Watch. The *Aberdeen Chronicle* of 2 December 1816, made the following comment:

'While we congratulate our fellow citizens on the establishment of an efficient watch throughout the City and the prospect of protection and security of the person and property of the lieges from the adoption of so necessary and salutory a measure, we have still the painful task of stating the continuance of the same alarming system of depredation to an extent wholly unprecedented.'

The Police Act of 1795 had made no provision for a Night-Watch and, although a new Act with such provision was in the course of preparation, it was decided to anticipate the Act by establishing a Night-Watch financed by public subscription. The committee members gave a hundred guineas, the Town Council fifty pounds while the magistrates made individual contributions. A total of three hundred and fifty pounds resulted. A public appeal was launched and citizens were urged to show, in tangible form, 'zeal and public spirit'.

Initially twenty men and a superintendent were engaged but within two months, the cost of running the Force was being questioned. It was held that four men for day duty and four for night, together with a superintendent, were sufficient for the burgh. A drastic reduction followed and, by the time the new Police Act came into being on 1 June 1818, this body had been reduced to seven men.

Chapter Two

1818-22

Charles Baird was the man on the spot when the Night-Watch was started on 1 June 1818. He had been in charge of the provisional force created by the Police Commissioners towards the end of 1816. The Commissioners regarded the new office — Superintendent of Watchmen — 'a very important situation which concerns the preservation of the public peace, the apprehension of offenders against the public tranquillity and the safety of the inhabitants'. They considered that Baird would 'befit the office well' and unanimously appointed him to the post. His weekly wage was increased from eighteen shillings to twenty-one, while the seven men under his command were to continue in office and receive eleven shillings weekly. Their duty was principally at night-time. The Force operated from the 'Watch-house', an old Guard House situated on the south side of Castle Street.

During the first week of the Force's existence, Superintendent Baird had to recruit a further two Watchmen for duty on Thursday, 4 June 1818 — the King's birthday and the anniversary of the unfortunate Castle Street riot, still very much in people's minds. As it happened, the next day was the occasion of a controversial public hanging, that of seventeen-year-old James Ritchie who had been sentenced to death for sheep-stealing in Morayshire; a demonstration was possible.

Ritchie had been arrested in January 1818 and accused of stealing thirty sheep from the Duke of Gordon's, Gordon Castle estate. At his trial, the jury had returned a unanimous verdict of guilty, but had added an earnest recommendation for mercy in view of the accused's extreme youth, the fact that it was his first conviction, and the possibility he had been the victim of a confidence gang. However, their rider was disregarded, as were the several petitions for clemency. Appeals were made direct to the Duke of Gordon, to whom the loss was negligible, but even his last minute attempt to obtain a reprieve failed, and the harsh justice of the time took its course. Ritchie was publicly hanged in Castle Street on 5 June, but instead of his body being given for dissection as was the custom, he was buried at sea.

A Night-Watchman *c.* 1818

By September 1818, the number of Watchmen controlled by the Commissioners had risen to twenty-four — Superintendent Baird and the following Watchmen whose names are recorded — George Gillan, Alexander Brown, Andrew Berrie, John Gray, Will Smith, John Walker, James Snowie, Alexander Johnstone, James Wilson, Gilbert Sutherland, Will Donald, James Fraser, James Allan, Andrew Ross, David Ross, Thomas Sutherland, Peter Sangster, George Crombie, Alexander Strath, Will Naughton, James Brown, George Smith and Peter McDonald. All were sworn in at a special sitting of the Quarter Sessions on 9 September 1818.

The Night-Watch experienced an early and unexpected set-back on 1 March 1819, when John Daniel, brushmaker, gave the Commissioners notice to quit the old Guard House in Castle Street, as he had purchased the site and desired immediate access to it. However, Daniel offered the Force alternative accommodation nearby and it appears to have been accepted. It remained in use till 1820, when the new courthouse building in Castle Street was opened. In Huxter Row, at the rear of the new building, accommodation was provided for a Watch-house.

Then, as now, one of the hazards of a policemen's life is his exposure to physical assaults on his person. To Robert Reid, a sailor, goes the doubtful honour of being the first person to have assaulted a policeman in Aberdeen! On 10 October 1818, he was fined two pounds for assaulting the Superintendent.

As mentioned before, the Night-Watchmen were employed by the Commissioners and performed duty during the hours of darkness. In the daytime law enforcement was still undertaken by the Town Sergeants, who were responsible to the Magistrates and Town Council. The Watchmen with their top coats, Tam o'Shanter bonnets and cudgels, were generally considered to be inferior to the Town Sergeants and referred to as 'Charlies'. The Town Sergeants also considered their creation an unwarranted intrusion into their affairs. Consequently, it was not uncommon for their respective employers — the Police Commissioners and the Magistrates — to criticise each other's Forces and this focused attention on the shortcomings of dual control! The jealousy between the two Forces manifested itself in another assault on Superintendent Baird. Because he had intervened in a quarrel between two Town Sergeants he had been attacked and made the target for abusive and insulting language. The outcome was that the Town Sergeants were each fined five pounds, but as provided for in the Aberdeen Police Act of 1818, two pounds of the fine was awarded to Baird in compensation for the 'considerable injury to his mouth'. The culmination of this 'outrage so gross' was a succinct notice in the *Aberdeen Journal:* 'The Magistrates have suspended John Roger from acting in the capacity of a Town Sergeant in consequence of an attack made by him on the Superintendent of Watchmen.'

However, it would seem that the incident served to improve relations between the rival Forces and led to better co-operation. This was reflected in an unusual case which occurred in August 1819 — one of conspiracy — the first of its kind in Scotland for over a century.

The case came to the notice of the authorities in the early hours of 3 August 1819. A watchman on duty in the Gallowgate was approached by a resident there, George Watson, a cooper, who complained that his house had been burgled and that the thief in his opinion was still on the premises. Another watchman joined them and the three went to Watson's house. They searched it thoroughly but no trace was found of the alleged intruder. However, the house was in a state of disorder, a window had been broken and its lower sash removed. Watson alleged that a red leather wallet containing two one pound notes had been stolen, adding that he suspected a neighbour John Hamilton. He next suggested that Simon Grant, a well known 'thief-catcher', should be sent for to search Hamilton's house. The watchmen ignored the suggestion but Watson contacted Grant himself, who, after preliminary investigation, refused to carry out the search. Watson then persuaded another Town Sergeant, George Campbell who was less experienced in criminal matters than Grant, to search Hamilton's house and the 'stolen' wallet was found under a bed.

Hamilton was, of course, arrested but subsequent enquiries revealed a conspiracy between Watson and a sixteen-year-old country youth, George Barron, to frame Hamilton for the burglary. Barron had gone to Hamilton's house and surreptitiously 'planted' the wallet under the bed whilst Watson himself had faked the burglary at his home. The motive in doing so was to have Hamilton, whom Watson disliked intensely, convicted for the crime. In those days, such a conviction would probably have incurred a lengthy sentence of imprisonment, transportation, or perhaps even death.

Watson might well have succeeded in framing Hamilton had it not been for the suspicions of the watchmen and the astuteness of Simon Grant. The latter had traced a woman who had overheard two men discussing the crime in a tavern, but unfortunately she had not been able to identify them. However, another witness was found who could — and the case was complete. Watson was convicted of conspiracy and sentenced to fourteen years' transportation.

In November 1819, the Commissioners decided to introduce a greater degree of supervision into the Night-Watch force by appointing a two-man patrol to cover the whole town during the night and for 'dispersing lay-abouts and ascertaining that the watchmen were doing their duty'. They also introduced an incentive scheme, whereby rewards were paid to watchmen who were instrumental in recovering stolen property, the circumstances being published in the local press. Two years later, in a further effort to improve the effectiveness of their Force, the Commissioners imposed more stringent disciplinary measures.

The familiar saying, 'You can't find a policeman when you want one', might well have been directed at the watchmen of 1822 just as it is to his counterpart today. However, one exception was the citizen who, towards midnight one night in January of that year, heard a woman screaming in the flat below his own. 'Murder! murder! let me be!' He rushed into the street and was fortunate enough to find a watchman. Both went immediately to the flat occupied by a Mr and Mrs William Gordon. Unable to gain access, they forced the door and found Mrs Gordon on her knees. Her cries became fainter and then stopped. A doctor was called but Mrs Gordon was found to be dead from a wound in the femoral artery. Only her husband was in the flat but he denied having assaulted his wife. He maintained she had fallen on the fender. However, the indications were that her injuries had been inflicted by a sharp pointed poker and Gordon was arrested and charged with murder. The jury found him guilty. He was sentenced to be hanged and his body given to the medical authorities for dissection.

The evidence led at the trial showed that both Gordon and his wife had been drunk at the time of the tragedy and, although petitions were organised for his reprieve and the jurors were associated in a recommendation for mercy, the sentence was carried out on the afternoon of 31 May 1822.

The subject of discipline among the watchmen caused problems for the Commissioners in March 1822, when they met to consider the circumstances of an assault on Watchman Magnus Lister by Robert Ingram. The Commissioners, having interviewed Magnus Lister and other watchmen who had been on duty at the time of the assault, as well as Superintendent Baird and Ingram, found:

'That although Lister had been so maltreated and abused as to be unable to go about duty for three nights after the assault took place, Mr Baird, for reasons best known to himself, neglected to prosecute

Ingram in terms of the Act of Parliament or even to make any record of the circumstances in his report book.'

The Commissioners were unanimous in their opinion that Baird was unfit for the situation of Superintendent of Watchmen and should be immediately dismissed from the service of the Board. He was called before the meeting and told his services were no longer required. The Clerk to the Commissioners confirmed the Board's decision in writing and in lieu of notice Baird received two weeks pay and an allowance of five pounds.

But what of Ingram? He was given the alternative of paying Magnus Lister three guineas in compensation for the injury which he had sustained, or being dealt with by the Magistrates. He paid the three guineas!

Thus Superintendent Baird's term of office came to an abrupt and unhappy end. No doubt, like the holder of any new office, he had numerous difficulties to overcome, yet such progress as was made during the first few years was in no small measure due to his efforts.

Chapter Three

1822-30

'WANTED! a steady, active man, with sober and attentive habits as Superintendent of the City Watchmen.' So read an advertisement in the *Aberdeen Chronicle* of 16 March 1822. It failed, however, to get a replacement for ex-Superintendent Baird. A letter was then written to Sir Richard Birnie of London, the famous Bow Street Magistrate, asking him to recommend one of his officers for the post. Sir Richard, who was a native of Banff and a saddler by trade, was held in high esteem throughout the country. He had particularly distinguished himself in 1820 leading a contingent at the arrest in London of the armed 'Cato Street Conspirators' — criminals in a big way who had planned to murder Cabinet Ministers, capture the Bank of England and the Mansion House, set fire to London and install a provisional government.

Sir Richard's first reply to the Commissioners was direct and to the point — the right type of man was not available at the salary offered. However, on 26 April 1822, he wrote to Provost Hadden that one of his Bow Street Officers, Robert Chapman, would be prepared to take the post and as a result the Commissioners held a special meeting on 4 May 1822, when the following resolution was passed unanimously — 'To put the superintendence of the watchmen under the charge of Chapman, having the fullest reliance on Sir Richard's recommendation, but upon the understanding that his engagement shall, in the first instance, be for one year; that the appointment shall be annually thereafter in May, and that he shall only be continued so long as he affords that satisfaction to the Commissioners which the good opinion of Sir Richard gives them reason to anticipate.' The canny Aberdonians were taking no chances!

The Commissioners then fixed the Superintendent's salary at one hundred pounds per annum, to which the Magistrates agreed to add twenty pounds yearly from the 'Rogue Money' account. The Board also agreed to pay Chapman's removal expenses by sea from London to Aberdeen.

At this time there appears to have been a built-in resistance by the public to entrust watchmen with sufficient powers to carry out their duties. Many felt deeply that the powers required would impinge on the liberty of the individual, consequently watchmen had to tread warily. Wrongful arrest might result in their being sued for damages, which they could ill afford to pay.

A good example of this occurred in Aberdeen shortly after Superintendent Chapman assumed control. In July 1822, Mr Alexander Shand, a local merchant, lodged a complaint with the Superintendent:

'Sir,
I hereby authorise you to apprehend and detain G. J. Mears of London, as a swindler and impostor, he having obtained from me the sum of £5 sterling under false pretences. I, at the same time, guarantee you from any responsibility in having interfered in the matter.

I am, etc.
(Signed) Alexander Shand.'

It was midnight when Superintendent Chapman received the complaint and, as there was a possibility that Mr Mears might leave town, it was obvious that immediate action had to be taken. However, before doing so the Superintendent checked the authenticity of the complaint and conferred with the Town Clerk. Mears was then arrested and detained overnight in the Watch-house and was given the Superintendent's bed! In the morning the Procurator-Fiscal was undecided on what to do and referred the matter to Dr Dauney, the Town's Legal Consultor and Sheriff-Substitute. The latter decided that there was insufficient evidence on which to take court action and decreed that Mears be released. This was done and Mears returned the disputed five pounds to Mr Shand. He then gave the Superintendent the following certificate:

19th July 1822.

'This certifies that Mr Robert Chapman having arrested me by the request of Mr Alexander Shand and the circumstances which gave rise to that arrest being perfectly cleared up, I hereby exonerate Mr Chapman from having taken any part in the transaction.

(Signed) G. J. Mears.'

The next morning Dr Dauney publicly rebuked Superintendent Chapman for wrongfully arresting Mears and not surprisingly, the Superintendent resented the rebuke, especially when it had been given before the Town Sergeants! He reported the matter to the Commissioners and asked for a clear explanation of his powers in such circumstances. He threatened to resign if 'Dr Dauney or any other high official character' ridiculed him again in public. The Commissioners gave Superintendent Chapman their full support describing Dr Dauney's comments as 'ill-mannered and uncalled for'.

A rather unusual section of the Watchmen's Regulations provided that gratuities could be paid to watchmen for 'praiseworthy service beyond the ordinary line of duty', but alas, such was the limited state of the Commissioners' funds that these gratuities were very seldom paid. However, in January 1825, there was a pleasing development, when the Magistrates agreed to make available for this purpose, part of the fines paid by delinquents brought before them by the Superintendent.

At this time there came into being other means of augmenting the watchmen's meagre earnings, which had remained constant from the outset. As it happened, the means then employed came to be regarded in later years as unorthodox and illegal. For example, as an encouragement to watchmen to detect persons responsible for committing nuisances in the streets on Saturday nights, it was decided to give the proceeds of the fines imposed to the watchmen concerned. Another method was to return unclaimed money, after intimation of its being found had been published in the newspapers. By this means Watchman William Jamieson in August 1827, collected thirty-eight pounds, the equivalent of eighteen months' pay! Early in the same year, the Watchhouse was fitted with gas lighting — a notable step towards efficiency!

A disturbance in Castle Street in August of that year involving Watchman Peter Stewart and several officers of the 25th Regiment then stationed in the Barracks brought into the open an aspect of Superintendent Chapman's character hitherto unsuspected. The incident in which Stewart was involved, and for which he was imprisoned on charges of assault and maltreatment, attracted the attention of one of the Commissioners, who went to the Watch-house to discuss the matter with the Superintendent. The latter could not be traced but when eventually contacted, was found to be 'in a state of extreme intoxication'. Rumour had it that such conduct was not uncommon! The Superintendent was suspended *sine die* and a committee appointed to report on the matter. The upshot was that the Commissioners accepted a written apology from Superintendent Chapman, but warned him that any recurrence would result in his immediate dismissal.

It will be recalled that the watchmen worked at night and went off duty at six in the morning. Their value as a crime prevention force was widely recognised, not least by a section of the criminal fraternity who confined their housebreaking activities to the period between six and seven o'clock on Sunday mornings, after the watchmen had gone home and before the majority of the inhabitants were abroad. To meet this situation, watchmen undertook extended duty till seven o'clock on Sunday mornings.

The Town Sergeants were still responsible for providing a Day Patrole to keep order in the streets, but in view of the fact that at no time were there more than six of them, and that they had many other duties to perform, little time was devoted to patrolling the streets. Consequently it is not surprising there was a feeling afoot that a regular day patrol would sooner or later become a necessity. This belief was undoubtedly shared by 'A Shopkeeper, Broad Street' who, on 11 October 1827, sent this letter to the *Aberdeen Chronicle*:

'Sir,
    I wish you would, through the medium of your very useful paper, direct the attention of the Police to a nuisance which is severely felt by many. I allude to those insane vagrants who are constantly perambulating our streets, much to the annoyance of the orderly part of the community. There are two in particular — one known by the name "Johnnie Macamfee" and another by that of "Feel Jamie". They are both constantly in a state of intoxication and when irritated as they frequently are by the boys in the streets, become highly dangerous. I have seen one of these maniacs throwing stones in Union Street, not three days ago, in such a way as to endanger the lives of passengers; and I myself have had, by one of the above-mentioned individuals, three panes of glass broken in my shop door, every one of which cost me 7s. to replace. Surely such things have only to be represented in the proper quarter to be redressed. At this moment, I hear G—— P——, another drunken character, roaring in my neighbourhood, with a crowd of black-guard boys about him, creating a disturbance which ought not to be allowed, where people pay for protection from such gross annoyance. By giving this room in an early number, you will oblige.'

The year 1829 was one of progress. In October, the Police Court came into being and on 12 November, the Commissioners established 'The Day Patrole'. It was drawn from watchmen 'who had conducted themselves with the greatest propriety' and comprised one sergeant

Chief Constable Wyness
1880–1902

Chief Constable Anderson
1903–32

Chief Constable McConnach
1933–55

Chief Constable Matheson
1955–63

Chief Constable Smith
1963–70

Chief Constable Morrison
1970–

Deputy C.C. MacQueen
(Acting C.C. Mar.–Sept. 1963)

Deputy C.C. Nicol
(Acting C.C. July–Nov. 1970)

and six men — Thomas Copland, John Gordon, Arthur Duff, Hughes Skinner, John Middleton and William McRobb under the charge of Watchman Alexander Fraser, who was appointed sergeant.

The Day Patrole was on duty from 6 a.m. until 9 p.m. with two one-hour breaks for meals. The Night-Watch covered the period from nine o'clock at night till six o'clock in the morning. Of the two, the Commissioners considered that The Day Patrole had to perform more exacting duties and should be paid at a higher rate than the night-watchmen. Accordingly, they fixed their earnings at fourteen shillings weekly and the sergeant's at sixteen shillings. They also provided them with great coats and batons which they purchased, in true Aberdeen tradition, 'at the lowest possible terms'.

The Regulations for The Day Patrole (Appendix v) laid down that the patrole-men should at all times be 'extremely attentive to sobriety and temperance'. Moreover they were not allowed to keep a public house or enter one except in the course of duty, or to ask for a New Year's gift from any inhabitant. They were required to be 'active, diligent, calm, civil, obliging, firm, steady and unbiased' while their spiritual well-being too was catered for by special arrangements being made for their attendance at church on Sundays and fast days.

Reference is also made in the Regulations to 'pocket-pickers, beggars, ballad-singers, the transport of whale blubber and to the arrival and departure of steam-boats and stage-coaches'. These serve as interesting reminders of the times.

In April 1830, Catherine Davidson or Humphrey murdered her husband, and was executed in October, the first occasion for forty-five years that a woman was publicly hanged in the city.

The case is not without interest. Her husband was a butcher, who, together with his wife, kept a public house in the city. Both were heavy drinkers and their relationship had never been good. She had, frequently and openly, threatened to cut his throat or poison him and in fact her husband had forecast that one day she would 'die looking down Marischal Street'.

The chief witness at the trial was a woman servant who lived with them. She told how on the night the crime was committed, Mrs Humphrey had told her to go to bed first — a most unusual occurrence. She also told how her mistress, *with a smile on her face*, had awakened her and said the master was ill. She also testified to the presence in the kitchen where her master slept, of oil of vitriol, a deadly corrosive poison, and related how her master had made, at various times between the night of Friday, when he was taken ill and Sunday when he died,

C

Day-Patrole Men *c.* 1840

remarks such as 'I'm burned — I'm gone — I'm roasted', and to his wife, 'Oh! Woman, woman, you have tried to do this often and you have done it now'. Oddly enough however, when the minister who was called to his bedside, asked him if his wife were responsible, he replied, 'No! No!'

She was found guilty and indeed after the trial, she admitted having administered to her husband the oil of vitriol whilst he slept — with his mouth open!

Today, it is rather puzzling to note the attitude of early members of the Force towards prisoners in their care. It certainly was contradictory, for on one hand they permitted some prisoners *en route* from the court-house to the prison to obtain alcoholic drink, whilst on the other they often kept them for days in the cells without food! Both practices were frowned upon by the Commissioners. Superintendent Chapman and Day-Patrole McRobb were reproved for allowing the prisoners to get drink and definite instructions were given to the Superintendent to ensure that Watch-house prisoners were given coarse bread and soup in the mornings before court.

In July 1830, Superintendent Chapman became the subject of a searching investigation following a complaint of assault and ill-treatment by Mr Daniel, a preacher of languages. The outcome of the enquiry is contained in a resolution passed unanimously by the Commissioners:

'1 That the conduct of Mr Chapman in violently pushing Mr Daniel from him, by which he fell upon the floor of the Watch-house was a gross violation of the third schedule of his regulations which prescribes that "he shall at all occasions maintain a calm, civil, obliging but firm and steady, conduct." '

2 That the conduct of Mr Chapman in recommending Mr Daniel to give money to the watchmen previous to his liberation, is unauthorised by the Board and highly censorable, as such a practice might be an inducement to the watchmen to apprehend citizens without just cause, for the purpose of obtaining money.'

In consequence of the resolution, Chapman tendered his resignation, which was to take effect from 29 October 1830, approximately eight and a half years from the date of his appointment. However, he was released on 2 October 1830, in order to escort convicts to London.

Notwithstanding the various problems which arose during his term of office, the Night-Watch and The Day Patrole developed considerably under Superintendent Chapman's direction. Night Patrole-man George Gillan, one of the Night-Watch pioneers, was appointed to act as *interim* Superintendent until a successor was found for Superintendent Chapman.

By now each member of The Day Patrole had been provided with 'a suit of clothes in blue cloth, tippets of oilcloth for wear during wet weather and a hat with patent glazed cover'. The suit of clothes and hat, conformed to the pattern adopted by the police in London and cost five pounds.

Chapter Four

1830-35

Mr John Fyfe was appointed to the vacant post of Superintendent of Watchmen. The formalities were dispensed with for the Commissioners knew their man. His integrity and high moral principles were indisputable and, moreover, he had been a King's Messenger and Sheriff Officer. They felt sure his example alone would reduce the incidence of drunkenness and indiscipline in the Night-Watch. So, on 18 October 1830, only sixteen days after Chapman had left Aberdeen, Superintendent Fyfe took command.

Fyfe's humanitarian principles soon became evident. In November, he obtained the Commissioners' consent to purchase a handcart 'for the conveyance to the Watch-house of persons found in an extreme state of intoxication in the streets'. In his view, it was undignified for the helplessly drunk to be dragged or carried bodily through the streets — and it was an unnecessarily strenuous task for some of the older members of the Force!

However, an even more momentous development occurred in December of that year. The first police doctor was appointed. For this alone, Superintendent Fyfe deserves to be remembered, for he succeeded in creating this post at a time when the slightest increase in expenditure was subjected to the most severe scrutiny.

Fyfe proposed to the Commissioners that they appoint a 'Medical Gentleman' who was prepared to come to the Watch-house at any time, by day or night, to attend emergency cases and to visit sick or disabled watchmen in their homes.

The Commissioners agreed, emphasising the desirability that the appointee should be on call at all times and, should he be absent for any reason, nominate a locum. They also decided that his salary should be five guineas for the first year — to be met from the revenue accruing from fines imposed in the Police Court — exclusive of any remuneration obtained from persons of means, whom he might be called upon to attend, or from the Procurators-Fiscal of the city or county, who required his services.

Dr. Francis Ogston, First Police Doctor 1830–80

Three city doctors applied for the position and, when the Commissioners met on 29 December 1830, a ballot was taken and a Dr Francis Ogston was duly elected to the post of Police Medical Attendant.

In spite of Superintendent Fyfe's warnings, some of his men still regarded occasional drinks from publicans as a legitimate perquisite, even when they were on duty. This was particularly true of members of the Night-Watch! It was not surprising, therefore, that with the approach of the New Year, 1831, the Superintendent asked his three night 'Patroles' to be diligent in their supervision of the watchmen and it must have been a bitter disappointment to him that two of the 'Patroles' themselves had to be dismissed for drunkenness on 10 January 1831.

Notwithstanding the poor pay and conditions of the Night-Watch, there appears to have been little difficulty in recruiting the authorised number of watchmen. An interesting feature of the times, and indeed of most of the nineteenth century, was the existence of supernumaries — a body of men who gathered nightly at the Watch-house door, eager to take the place of any watchman who might be indisposed. They were prepared to do a night's watch for as little as one shilling and sixpence.

Superintendent Fyfe rightly believed the supernumaries were not the best source of recruitment and persuaded the Commissioners to advertise in the newspapers for watchmen, stipulating a preference for married men and excluding pensioners. An indication of the establishment of the Night-Watch at this period is given in Appendix VI — a reproduction of the 'Roll of Watchmen on Duty: 17 and 18th July, 1831'. It details the names and stations (beats) of the twenty-eight watchmen on duty that night, headed by the names of the three 'Patroles'.

A body-snatching scare hit Aberdeen with devastating effect on Monday, 19 December 1831. A mob, which at one stage reached ten or twelve thousand citizens, set fire to the then recently built Anatomical Theatre in St Andrew Street. Provost Hadden, the Magistrates, The Day Patrole, Town Sergeants and men of the 79th Regiment from Castlehill Barracks were called to the scene, but such was the frenzied state of the mob, that the forces of law and order dared not oppose it lest bloodshed result. The 'Riot Act' was read by Provost Hadden — actually the last occasion in which it was done in Aberdeen — but of course, it was not enforced as it was decided to allow the mob to achieve its limited objective — the destruction of the Anatomical Theatre or 'Burkin' Hoose' and everything connected with it.

The reason underlying the riot lay, not in Aberdeen, but in Edinburgh, where, during 1827 and 1828, two Irishmen, William Burke and William Hare had murdered at least fifteen people and sold their bodies to the anatomists. It is not surprising, therefore, that any activity savouring of 'Burke and Hare-ism' was viewed everywhere with deep suspicion, Aberdeen being no exception.

In 1831, the newly erected Dr Andrew Moir's Anatomical Theatre in St Andrew Street had only just got going as a school of anatomy, when destruction befell it.

A dog had unearthed a fragment of a human body from ground at the rear of the building and had carried it into the street. Two young lads 'took over' from the dog and, with a crowd around them, dug up further human remains. The crowd grew. An ugly situation developed and Dr Moir and his students were obliged to run from the building, Dr Moir to his lodgings, from which he had later to escape through a back window!

Within the 'Burkin' Hoose' the crowd found three mangled corpses, which were taken outside. The sight of these drove a section of the crowd berserk! There were cries of 'Burn the house!' and 'Down with the Burkin' Shop!' Some fetched combustible materials and set fire to the building, whilst others undermined and battered down the walls. The falling in of the roof brought resounding cheers from the crowd.

Three rioters, Andrew Murray, George Sharpe and Alexander Allan were subsequently indicted for (1) Mobbing and Rioting; (2) Fire-raising and Destruction of Property, and (3) Assault and putting the Lieges in a State of Fear and Alarm. They all pleaded guilty to the first charge and were each sentenced to a year's imprisonment. The other charges were dropped. The court felt that the 'Medical Gentlemen', although carrying out a legitimate activity, had contributed to the riot by their own carelessness, while it was felt that the prisoners had not been the ring-leaders of the insurrection.

The ever-increasing problem of drunkenness in the community, in particular the number of persons found on the streets suffering from the effects of intoxication or exposure to the cold, received the enlightened attention of Superintendent Fyfe and Dr Ogston during 1832, when the following items were procured, 'a new stomach pump on the most improved principles, cell blankets and tin hot-water bottles to counter the ill-effects of alcoholism and to aid in the restoration of circulation and body heat to persons in a state of insensibility'.

Again in 1832 and in the succeeding years, money, or more correctly the lack of it, was to figure prominently in the affairs of The Day

Patrole and Night-Watch. It was to the discredit of the Commissioners and the Magistrates that they quibbled over the financial arrangements, for not only did their haggling adversely affect the personnel, but also the community as a whole.

The difficulty began in February. The Commissioners, hard pressed for funds to meet their many improvement projects, asked the Magistrates to contribute towards the upkeep of The Day Patrole from 'Rogue Money' funds. However, some of the Magistrates still felt that their Town Sergeants were adequate for day-time duty and the request for financial assistance was turned down. The Commissioners, in return, threatened to disband The Day Patrole.

Members of the public reacted swiftly. A petition was drawn up protesting against the disbandment on economic grounds of The Day Patrole. Signed by several hundred citizens, it concluded with these words: 'the under-signed entrust that the Commissioners will abandon all thoughts of diminishing the efficiency of an establishment which has been of great utility in this City.'

By way of retaliation the Commissioners raised their economy axe over the Night-Watch and informed Superintendent Fyfe they proposed to reduce the manpower of the force on 1 April. The Superintendent, in his usual forthright manner, put the ball squarely back in the Commissioners' court, with the submission: 'that as the number of Watchmen was to be reduced on 1st April ensuing, the Watch Committee (a term which appears to have come into being about this time) might fix the various rounds, as he did not consider himself equal to the task.'

The submission had the desired effect and the Superintendent was directed to continue the present number of men until further notice. Thereafter, the Watch Committee interviewed members of The Day Patrole and Night-Watch regarding a possible curtailment of its strength, but concluded that no reduction should take place.

The Town Sergeants, who had long since learned to live with and tolerate the Night-Watch, now began to see The Day Patrole as a greater threat to their existence. This fear was expressed in an article by one of them in the *Aberdeen Herald* of February 1837. The article complained 'that The Day Patrole wished to engross the whole of the criminal duty to themselves and that when the sergeants had a case in hand, the Patrole endeavoured to throw every obstacle in their way'.

A Committee was appointed to investigate the difficulties and it reported that the Town Sergeants with their various duties, civil as well as criminal, could not consistently provide an effective Day

Patrole and that their duties should be confined exclusively to those required of them by the Magistrates. The report further recommended that the best understanding should exist between the Town Sergeants and The Day Patrole and that one should not interfere with the prisoners of the other. It was felt also that the situation would be helped if the Town Sergeants were provided with a 'lock-up room' for their prisoners so that they would not be obliged to use the Watch-house cells.

Like the earlier dispute with the Town Sergeants, some good did result. The Magistrates agreed to contribute one hundred and five pounds annually from 'Rogue Money' funds to help defray the cost of The Day Patrole. With this development, the Commissioners agreed to increase the strength of The Day Patrole to seven. However, Superintendent Fyfe did not benefit from the slightly improved financial situation, although his responsibilities and those of The Day Patrole and Night-Watch had increased considerably since he took office. When he asked for an increase in salary, not only did the Commissioners refuse it, they actually considered reducing it, owing to the poor state of their funds! A burst of generosity followed and in March 1835, as a gesture towards Superintendent Fyfe's good and faithful service, the Commissioners agreed to allow him to purchase a writing desk!

The failure of the Commissioners to improve the conditions of himself and his men continued to cause the Superintendent grave concern, a situation which might have continued indefinitely had not a tragic accident befallen one of his men on 26 October 1835.

Early that morning, Watchman Joseph Collie, returning from duty in Waterloo Quay 'during most tempestuous weather' was blown into the dock and drowned. He left a widow and young family in very destitute circumstances. On 16 November 1835, the Superintendent raised the question of a gratuity for Collie's widow. The Commissioners agreed to make an award, but the meagreness of it deeply shocked the Superintendent. Consequently, it came as no surprise that at a meeting of the Board of Commissioners, on 4 December 1835, there was laid before them a letter from Mr Fyfe in which he resigned his office as Superintendent of the City Watchmen. He gave no reason.

The Board accepted Fyfe's resignation, without comment, and once again appointed night patrole-man George Gillan to act as *interim* Superintendent until a successor to Superintendent Fyfe was found.

Chapter Five

1836-39

The problem which beset the Watch Committee was how best to fill Superintendent Fyfe's shoes. Were the responsibilities too much for one man? The Committee obviously thought so and recommended to the Commissioners that two Superintendents be appointed, one for The Day Patrole and one for the Night Watch, at annual salaries of fifty-five and seventy-five pounds respectively.

The outcome was that on 15 February 1836, William Walker was appointed Superintendent of the seven-men strong Day Patrole and on 4 April, Lieutenant Robert Alexander of the Edinburgh Police was selected to fill the post of Superintendent of Watchmen, the office vacated by Superintendent Fyfe.

However, within a few months, it was realised that the division of responsibilities was unsatisfactory and accordingly the regulations of both bodies were amended to give the Superintendent of Watchmen overall control, whenever necessary.

A major problem then confronting the city authorities was the plight of the poor children, aptly described as being 'in a state of degradation worthy only of a pagan community'. In this connection the city was indeed fortunate in having in Sheriff-Substitute William Watson a man dedicated to improve the lot of neglected and under-privileged children — a work which earned for him the title 'The Children's Sheriff'.

The Sheriff's reforming zeal was confined not only to children; the friendless and destitute of all ages benefited from his work. With financial support from George Watt, a local doctor, and other public benefactors, his energies in the early thirties were directed towards the provision of a 'House of Refuge' and in September 1836 such an establishment was opened in the Guestrow.

One of the first to benefit from the 'House of Refuge' scheme was a Major Bennet, late of the 5th Foot Regiment, who had fallen on hard times. He had been rescued from the harbour by watchmen and there was reason to believe he had attempted to take his own life. Police

Commissioner Thomas Burnett — the man who had been largely responsible for bringing the Night-Watch into being twenty years before — took an active interest in Bennet and helped his rehabilitation.

In January 1837, the Commissioners appear to have been in a more generous frame of mind. They increased Doctor Ogston's salary from five to ten guineas and procured for The Day Patrole, white hats and coat buttons inscribed with 'Aberdeen Police'. But this generosity was short lived! In May, the haggling re-commenced, the Magistrates being the instigators. They resolved to discontinue the annual grant from 'Rogue Money' funds to The Day Patrole. The Commissioners immediately protested that without it The Day Patrole could not be maintained and decided to disband the Force, 'leaving with the Magistrates and Council the responsibility of preserving the peace and of apprehending delinquents to which they are bound by the Common Law of the Country'.

The disbandment of The Day Patrole took place on 20 June 1837, and to the six already over-burdened Town Sergeants fell the additional duty of providing a day-time patrol.

Superintendent Alexander had no wish to lose the services of the seven redundant men and persuaded the Commissioners to allow the retention — as an adjunct to the Night Watch — of the four most efficient of them, including the former Superintendent William Walker. His foresight was appreciated several months later when, as a result of public pressure, it was agreed to employ watchmen on day duty, as and when the situation demanded. This arrangement prevailed until 15 October 1838, when The Day Patrole was re-established. This time it consisted of Superintendent Walker and five men, paid at the reduced rate of ten shillings and sixpence weekly.

The night of 7 October 1838, proved to be the blackest in the history of the Night-Watch. Christopher Brown, labourer, of Printfield near Aberdeen, had been drinking in a public house in Exchequer Row and left there about nine o'clock. Thereafter, nothing is known of his movements until midnight, when he was arrested in the Gallowgate by Watchman William McDonald. However, Brown escaped from McDonald's custody, ran along the Gallowgate and West North Street where McDonald caught up with him, viciously assaulting him and inflicting injuries from which Brown subsequently died.

In 1839, at the spring sitting of the High Court, McDonald was tried for murder. The indictment against him stated that 'on the night of the 7th or morning of the 8th October, last, you did feloniously assault Christopher Brown, by throwing him to the ground, striking him with your baton, jumping violently on his belly with your knees whereby his liver was ruptured and his gall bladder detached from his liver, so that he was mortally wounded and died in consequence of his wounds'.

Unhappily, the case against McDonald was proved by the testimony of fellow watchmen and other witnesses. For the prosecution, the Advocate-Depute asked for a verdict of culpable homicide instead of murder and McDonald's Counsel agreed. The jury was asked to recommend mercy on account of the prisoner's previous good character, but the jury, while returning a verdict of culpable homicide, did not recommend mercy. The judge, Lord Cockburn, gave his view, that because of the suggestion contained in some of the evidence that the prisoner had been motivated by robbery, the gravity of the charge and the fact that McDonald had been employed to protect the lieges, the sentence of transportation for life was justified.

A sequel to the case was a petition for aid presented to the Commissioners by Christopher Brown's widow. The matter was referred to the Law Agents who ruled that there was nothing in the Police Act to authorise the Commissioners to make any allowance to the widow and a reply to that effect was sent to Mrs Brown.

The whole question of the Force's discipline now came under consideration. It would appear that Superintendent Alexander's own behaviour was somewhat unorthodox; he is said to have been in the habit of receiving prisoners reclining comfortably on a sofa! Accordingly, the Commissioners became concerned and on 28 November 1838, decided that, with immediate effect and for a period of three months, the watchmen would receive military drill for periods of one hour three times weekly.

The decision was highly unpopular and at the first parade, thirty-nine of the watchmen objected! A fortnight later, one of the watchmen was suspended for drunkenness on parade and, finally, towards the end of December, the watchmen presented a petition to the Commissioners protesting against the drill. After consideration, it was decided to discontinue the experiment. The men's main objection was more monetary than physical — there was no extra pay for parades, yet the Commissioners appeared to have been unable to see the men's point of view.

However, the discontinuance of the parades certainly disappointed the public, who had little in the way of entertainment and thoroughly enjoyed the spectacle of strapping young men of six feet and over, marching alongside old men, some barely five feet in height!

In March 1839, the Commissioners were called upon to investigate a complaint by Alexander Cadenhead, the Procurator-Fiscal, that Superintendent Alexander had used improper means to obtain a confession. It was alleged he had promised alcoholic drink to a woman if she would give information as to how she came into possession of certain articles of property. The matter was referred to the Watch Committee for investigation and it was found that the Superintendent had acted improperly and imprudently. They accepted his explanation: that it had been done in a jocular manner without consideration of the consequences.

The Day Patrole with its full muster of six men was now much too small to be effective. Even the combined resources of The Patrole and the Town Sergeants meant that only twelve men could be mustered during the day to enforce the law — not many, when one considers that Aberdeen's population was close on fifty-five thousand. It is not surprising therefore, that in the more crowded areas of the city such as Castle Street and vicinity, there were scenes of degradation such as would not be tolerated today.

The deplorable conditions which then existed in these areas were raised at a Town Council meeting by one of the Magistrates, who carried on business in the neighbourhood. He complained that the indecent and blasphemous language used by the large number of profligate and dissolute females who congregated in the area was such that not even servants could reasonably be exposed to it. Mason's Court (now Lodge Walk), he protested, had actually been taken possession of by prostitutes against the wishes of the proprietrix. Another member of the Council complained that it was disgusting to see so many beggars lying about the streets with open sores on their arms and legs.

The situation was taken in hand by Superintendent Alexander's men and the Town Sergeants, the offenders being 'moved on', but this was not the answer as they simply returned when the patrol left! Imprisonment was no deterrent either; indeed many of them actually welcomed it during the winter months.

A temporary remedy was found by a well-known east-end grocer, part of whose property had been occupied unlawfully by prostitutes and vagrants. It would seem that squatters are nothing new. At first, he removed the furniture, but this was quickly retrieved before it could be carted away. He then took off the doors and windows but this, too, had little effect. However, a water hose was acquired and when brought to bear on his unwelcome 'tenants', they fled from the building like half-drowned rats and stayed away long enough for the openings to be boarded up.

In May 1839, ill-health overtook Superintendent Alexander. The Commissioners reacted to the news with cold indifference, and unanimously passed the following resolution: 'that it would be greatly to the advantage of the Watch Department to have a more able, active and efficient Superintendent, who could exercise complete control over the inferior officers of the Department.'

When he heard of the resolution, Superintendent Alexander intimated that his health was improving, so the Commissioners agreed to let him continue in office for a further two months, the understanding being that he would demit office on three weeks' notice, should they require him to do so. Little wonder that on 23 September 1839, a special meeting of the Board of Commissioners was convened to receive a letter of resignation from Alexander. The letter read:

'Gentlemen,

'I find that the duties imposed upon me viz. to attend from 10 o'clock a.m. till 2 o'clock p.m. and thereafter from 7 o'clock p.m. till 6 o'clock a.m. the following morning when the men go off duty, is more than I, or any person, could be expected to attend to.

'I therefore feel myself under the necessity of resigning my situation as Superintendent of Police into your hands.

'I shall be prepared to leave at the end of three months from 1st October. By allowing me that time, it will enable me to look about for another situation.

and oblige, Gentlemen, etc.,

(Signed) Robert Alexander.

21st September, 1839

'P.S. I shall leave off duty at the end of three months from first of October, next.

(Signed) Robert Alexander.

23rd September, 1839.'

The Commissioners accepted the resignation and resolved to appoint a 'properly qualified person' to the post, without delay.

Chapter Six

1839-54

The Commissioners wasted no time in finding a successor to Superintendent Alexander and the Watch Committee met within a week of his resignation. They decided to advertise the post at a salary of one hundred and fifty pounds and to restrict applications to men under forty-five years of age. The successful applicant was Robert Barclay of the City of Glasgow Police, who took over from Alexander on 1 December 1839.

Barclay's arrival was marked by the provision of new greatcoats for The Day Patrole and the appointment of patrole-man Robert McKenzie to a new post, that of 'Criminal Officer' with special responsibility for investigation and supervision. The changes resulted in a dispute between the Commissioners and ex-Superintendent William Walker, now Sergeant of The Day Patrole. Several disciplinary charges were preferred against Walker and he resigned from the Force. He was replaced by Sergeant Alexander Weir from Dundee, whose duties were made subject to the control and direction of Superintendent Barclay. This sounded the death-knell of the experimental 'two Superintendents' system of previous years. To round off Barclay's first year of office, reconstruction work was begun at the Watch-house to provide three much needed new cells.

Although Barclay was well aware that some of the outer beats of the town were too large, it took a public enquiry into a disastrous fire at Footdee in December 1840, in which five people perished, to convince the Commissioners of the need for a larger Force.

The fire was indeed a tragedy. It occurred on a Wednesday night in December at the 'Victoria Tavern' in Knowles' timber yard — adjoining York Place at Footdee — the home of James Howie, his wife, two daughters and a boarder named Thomas Marshall.

Shortly after midnight, a watchman extinguished a street-lamp — one of their duties at that time — about thirty yards from the house, but saw no sign of fire. Shortly afterwards, however, some ships' carpenters raised the alarm and the watchmen, then in Links Street,

UNIFORMS
Watchman 1857 Constable 1897
Constables 1903

UNIFORMS
Constable 1925   Sergeant 1925
Inspector 1925   Constable 1971

Mounted Section 1937
(Formed 1899)

"Rennie" 1959

Pipe Band 1926
Pipe Band 1970
(Formed 1907)

hurried back to find dense smoke pouring from the roof and chimneys. Fire engines were called. Meanwhile, the ships' carpenters and watchmen tried to gain access to the upper floors where the residents slept, but were beaten back by the flames and smoke. Two hours later, when the fire was subdued, the charred remains of the hapless victims were found in the smouldering ruins.

Commenting on the fire, *The Aberdeen Journal* of 16 December 1840, reported:

'That the premises should have taken fire is not so much to be wondered at, but that all the human beings they contained should have perished without the slightest warning of their danger, does seem to be very extraordinary. . . . The occurrence of so distressing an event ought undoubtedly to enforce on all to whom the guardianship of the night is entrusted, the strictest vigilence, at all times. Considering the vast quantity of combustible materials at Footdee, and the multiplied chances of accidental fires in that quarter, the arrangements for watching it ought to be more extensive and complete.'

A public enquiry exonerated the watchmen but recommended an increase in their number in the area. Henceforth, a further two watchmen were employed at Footdee.

By the beginning of 1841, the House of Refuge in the Guestrow was well established and proving of great benefit to the community. However, Sheriff Watson did not rest upon his laurels. He next concentrated his energies on the plight of needy children. He shocked the community when he stated there were within the city two hundred and eighty children under fourteen without any means of subsistence other than by begging and stealing. He described as cruel and absurd the existing practice of sending children of from eight to eleven years of age to prison for these crimes, when it was apparent that only by doing so, could the vast majority of them survive.

The Sheriff's endeavours bore fruit and on 1 October 1841, the first Industrial School was opened in Chronicle Lane. It was a modest establishment with only ten pupils. The scholars were provided with breakfast, dinner and supper, in return for working hard: learning to read and write, net-making and teasing hair. They spent their nights in the hovels they called home.

The venture attracted attention of members of the Justiciary and Lord Cockburn, the well-known High Court judge, visited the school. It was the same Lord Cockburn who presided over the High Court in the spring of 1842 at the trial of Harris Rosenberg and his wife,

D

Alethia Rosenberg, described as 'foreigners'. They had been indicted for wilful fire-raising, the circumstances leading to their arrest coming to light between ten and eleven o'clock on the night of Saturday, 19 February 1842. A watchman was called to Rosenberg's shop — H. Rosenberg and Company, Manufacturing Furriers, 115 Union Street — where smoke was seen coming from a window. The watchman immediately went to the Rosenbergs' lodgings about two hundred and fifty yards distant, where he reported the circumstances to Rosenberg. When he failed to come out after five minutes, the watchman called Rosenberg again, but still he made no appearance and, after a further period of waiting, the watchman entered his bedroom. Rosenberg was still only partly dressed. Eventually they reached the shop and on entering saw flames passing through neatly bored holes in a wooden partition. Fortunately, the fire was of no great extent and it was easily extinguished.

Investigations followed and Harris Rosenberg was charged with wilful fire-raising. His odd behaviour when notified of the fire, the presence of a box of combustible materials and a cut gas pipe near the seat of the fire, together with other suspicious circumstances and the fact that the goods in the shop had been insured for twelve hundred pounds, when in fact, they were worth only two hundred and fifty, secured the conviction of Harris Rosenburg and his wife for wilful fire-raising. The former was sentenced to transportation for life; the latter received two years' imprisonment. An unusual feature of the Rosenberg trial was that it commenced on the morning of Saturday, 16 April 1842, and finished at twelve-thirty the following day, Sunday.

Several changes in the Force took place about this time: the resignation of Sergeant Weir and the appointment of Night-Watch patroleman John Watson in his place; the fitting of numerals to the overcoats of all personnel; the appointment at ten shillings a week of a woman attendant to search female prisoners; and the assumption, in 1844, by Superintendent Barclay of the additional duties as Superintendent of Fire Engines.

Although The Day Patrole and the Night-Watch were no longer independent units, the Commissioners were obviously determined to regard the day men as the more important. In a revision of the day Sergeant's remuneration, they fixed his annual salary at fifty-five pounds, while the pay of the Night-Watch Sergeant was twenty shillings weekly.

Sheriff Watson's already mentioned 'School of Industry' in Chronicle Lane was proving its worth and members of the public were now rallying to its support. In one appeal for aid, William Thom, 'The Inverurie Poet', himself an orphan boy wrote:

'Go to Chronicle Lane. Look carefully at these sharp little fellows and think of your own safety if nothing else. . . . In these hundred boys, as they are being trained, you have an equivalent for 100 patent locks, forty policemen, two transports and one hangman.'

A similar school for girls — also suggested by Sheriff Watson — was opened in Long Acre on 5 June 1843, and its initial success was largely due to public-spirited citizens like Miss Elizabeth Ogilvie, of the Ruthrieston family.

Early in May 1845, Sheriff Watson and others met to discuss the problem of juvenile delinquency. Superintendent Barclay reported to the meeting that, while the incidence of crime amongst young people was decreasing, he was concerned at the large number of young people begging in the streets who could not be compelled to attend school. The Sheriff suggested a remedy to the Magistrates — they should authorise the police to apprehend every child found begging, while he undertook to issue the necessary warrants.

On 9 May 1845, it was decided to implement this measure, and the Public Soup Kitchen in Loch Street was set aside for the reception of delinquents. By two o'clock that afternoon, sixty-five had been apprehended and were compulsorily stripped, bathed and fed. Of course, their relatives demonstrated outside, but dispersed on being told their children were at dinner and would be freed in the evening after supper. Before being sent home, the children were told if they gave an undertaking to give up begging, they could return the following day for similar treatment and training. All but four returned and so the 'kitchen' developed into a Juvenile Reformatory School.

The Sheriff's 'House of Refuge' in the Guestrow was also to play a greater part in the treatment of young offenders. On 4 August 1846, it was arranged that juvenile delinquents, instead of being taken to the Watch-house would be taken to the House of Refuge where the Prison Board would provide suitable accommodation for their reception, and where one of Superintendent Barclay's men would be in attendance to take charge of them.

By such constructive action, Sheriff Watson and his associates brought Aberdeen to the forefront in the country's efforts to curb crime among young people.

By the year 1847, Dr Francis Ogston's services as police doctor were in much greater demand, and his salary was raised to thirty guineas. The men benefited in that the doctor had now to provide free medical attention for the sick, as well as for injured, members of the Force, while another of his new duties was to examine all recruits prior to their appointment. Of course, sickness was not confined to the men. In November 1847, Superintendent Barclay fell ill and was almost continuously on sick leave until 1 August 1849, when he was required either to resume duty or resign. Sergeant John Watson deputised for him at an increased salary of sixty-five pounds plus a gratuity of fifteen pounds for the added responsibility.

Superintendent Barclay was a handsome, courageous man with a streak of vanity, who in trying to please all, actually pleased very few. He was fond of sport, horse-riding in particular, and a heavy throw at a steeple-chase is said to have had a detrimental effect on his health. Barclay's physical courage is proved by the story of how he personally chastised and humiliated a notorious character — a carter known as 'The Tearer'. One night 'The Tearer', who boasted he could 'thrash the whole Police establishment', reigned supreme in a public house in the Netherkirkgate. He had wrecked the furnishings, terrified the customers and was in the process of demanding drink of the publican, when the Superintendent walked in.

Barclay spoke sharply to 'The Tearer' who strongly resented the remarks. He attacked Barclay, as he had done other watchmen on previous occasions, but was no match for the wiry Superintendent. Barclay promptly tossed him on his back, on no fewer than six occasions, then told him, rather contemptuously, to go home when he had got back his breath. For some time after, 'The Tearer' was a very quiet man.

Monday, 12 March 1849, was indeed a sad day for the men. The Watch Committee, having just learned that the wage-bill for the previous year exceeded that of 1843 by nearly four hundred pounds, gave instructions for the imposition of drastic economies.

Wages were the first to suffer. The men's weekly pay was reduced: that of The Day Patrole men and the patrole-men of the Night-Watch was reduced from fifteen shillings to fourteen; that of the watchmen from twelve shillings to eleven; the Watch-house clerk's from fifteen shillings to twelve; and the female attendant's from ten shillings to eight. Even the sick benefit paid was curtailed. Hitherto, men who were off duty through illness, had received full pay for four weeks, followed by half pay for a similar period. Now, full pay was to be granted only to men who were off work on account of an injury sustained while on duty, and the others had to be content with half pay, and that for not more than four weeks in any one year.

By these economies, the Watch Committee estimated that a saving of one hundred and eighty pounds could be effected. However, they decided to re-open the old dispute with the Magistrates and Town Council relating to the payment of a grant from 'Rogue Money' funds in support of The Day Patrole.

The ever-present problem of drunkenness was again under consideration in 1849. There was no statute law whereby persons guilty of being drunk could be punished by a Magistrate. The usual procedure in dealing with the situation was to lodge drunken persons overnight in the Watch-house cells and release them in the morning without any charge being made against them. In March of that year, the Commissioners decided that 'drunks' who had money in their possession, should pay for their overnight accommodation! The arrangement was criticised by Sheriff Watson, who suggested that such persons should be reported to the Procurator-Fiscal as 'obstructors of thoroughfares' or 'breakers of the peace'.

In August 1849, Superintendent Barclay resumed duty after his long illness, Dr Ogston having certified that he was fit for day duties only. Accordingly, the Commissioners granted Barclay a new agreement whereby his salary was reduced from two hundred pounds to one hundred and fifty and from which he was obliged to pay the wages of a Night-Watch patrole-man to supervise the Force on his behalf.

That year, the rate of serious crime in Aberdeen and the North-East was exceptionally high. At the autumn sitting of the High Court, for example, eighteen cases were heard: four for murder, eleven for robbery and one each for rape, forgery and uttering base coin. One murderer was sentenced to be hanged; another to twenty years' transportation to Australia for culpable homicide; the third to twelve months' imprisonment and the fourth was found 'Not Proven'. The other criminals received sentences ranging from five to twenty years' transportation.

A feature of these High Court sittings and more particularly of executions, was the sale in the streets of sensational news sheets giving accounts — often fictitious — of the trials and, if appropriate, the condemned persons' dying confessions. The vendors paraded the streets shouting, 'Full and true account of the murder — Only one penny'; or 'The Murderer's dying confession — Only one penny'. To help promote sales, some even carried long poles bearing a grim picture of the execution.

A complaint in June 1852 by ex-Watchman Alexander Forbes made the news. He complained that Superintendent Barclay had withheld his share of 'Fire Money'. This highlights an interesting perquisite then enjoyed by the men: the practice of Insurance Companies covering outbreaks of fire, to pay agreed sums to the Superintendent of Police, for distribution amongst those who had been actively engaged in extinguishing the fires. It was reported that Forbes had indeed been present at a number of fires but had not been actively engaged in fire-fighting and in consequence had not been eligible for payment. Accordingly, his complaint was dismissed as being frivolous and vexatious.

On the evening of Monday, 4 October 1852, a brutal double murder took place at Kittybrewster, then just outwith the city boundary. The victims were Mrs Barbara Ross, an elderly lady, and her five-year-old grandson. They lived in a cottar-house on Peter McRobbie's farm, 'Sunnybank', Kittybrewster. The house adjoined McRobbie's barn, the key to which was kept by Mrs Ross.

At nine o'clock, McRobbie went to get the barn key. He was surprised to be met at the door by a man named George Christie, whom he recognised as a labourer employed by the contractor, whom he had engaged to thresh his crop in the barn. McRobbie's surprise gave way to concern when he heard what sounded like moans coming from the house, so he called upon a neighbour Mr Grant and together they returned to the cottar-house. They questioned Christie about the moans and he explained that the boy had a sore stomach. However, soon afterwards, McRobbie and Grant saw Christie lock the door and walk away with a bundle under his arm. They summoned Watchman Richardson of the County Police at Printfield and forced entry to the house. Here they found the dead and mutilated bodies of Mrs Ross and her grandson on the floor, and nearby an axe, which had evidently been used to kill the victims.

Three hours later, Richardson and Night-Watch patrole-man Nicol arrested Christie in a house at Denburn, Aberdeen, and when charged, he denied the crime. However, he was in possession of articles of property belonging to Mrs Ross and had blood on his shoes, trousers and shirt. Other items belonging to Mrs Ross were recovered later from a broker's shop, and Christie was identified as the seller.

George Christie stood trial at the High Court of Justiciary, Edinburgh, on Thursday, 23 December 1852. He was found guilty. After donning the black cap, The Lord Justice-Clerk said, 'In respect of the verdict above recorded, The Lord Justice-Clerk, Lords Cowan and Anderson discern and adjudge you, to be carried from the bar to the prison of Aberdeen, therein to be detained, and fed on bread and water only, till the 13th day of January next, and between 8 and 10 of the forenoon of that day ordain the said George Christie to be taken out of the said prison to the common place of execution, to be hanged by the neck on a gibbet till you be dead; and ordain your body to be buried within the precincts of the prison; and may God Almighty have mercy upon your soul.'

The sentence was carried out in conformity with the law and Christie was executed at eight-fifteen on the morning of Thursday, 13 January 1853.

Superintendent Robert Barclay died in office. His death on Wednesday, 29 March 1854, came as no surprise to his men, who, for some years, had witnessed a steady deterioration in his state of health. Despite this, he had held office for over fourteen years, twice as long as any of his predecessors, and under his direction the Force had grown in size and in stature. On 4 April 1854, The Commissioners minuted their appreciation of the able manner in which the late Mr Barclay had discharged the duties of his office and the deep regret felt by the community, now deprived of his valuable services.

Chapter Seven

1854-61

Sergeant John Watson — known as 'Muckle Watson' on account of his stature — had been a great help to Superintendent Barclay during his years of failing health. Indeed, for several lengthy spells from 1847 onwards, he had deputised for him. It therefore came as no surprise, when on 14 April 1854, the Commissioners selected him for the vacant post in preference to Superintendent Henry Williams of the Forfarshire Police. Mr William Anderson, Builder, Aberdeen, agreed to stand surety for Watson to the sum of one hundred and fifty pounds — one year's salary.

Superintendent Watson was a local product in that he was the first man to progress through the ranks, from night-watchman to Superintendent. He was tall and well built, his early life as a soldier reflecting in his military bearing. He was intelligent, understanding and possessed a keen sense of humour. On his appointment, it was widely acknowledged that he was the right man for the post. One of The Day Patrole men, Alexander Watson — known as 'Little Sandy' to distinguish him from his namesake — was appointed principal Sergeant in place of the Superintendent.

Prior to the year 1854, there were no regulations governing the conduct of public houses, indeed many of them never closed! However, in that year, the Public House Regulation Act — usually referred to as the 'Forbes McKenzie Act' after its sponsor — was passed. One of its main provisions was to introduce the principle of licensing hours, eleven o'clock at night being set as 'closing time' for both hotels and public houses. The Act also prohibited the sale of intoxicating liquor during hours of worship on Sundays.

The Act was by no means a popular piece of legislation. Nevertheless, the Commissioners and Magistrates felt the law must be upheld and Superintendent Watson was instructed to prosecute all offenders. Their enthusiasm for the Act was short-lived however, when David Robertson of the Royal Hotel was prosecuted and fined twenty-five shillings, for trading after eleven o'clock. The occasion was a celebration dinner given by the officers of the Royal Aberdeenshire Militia, to mark the presentation of new colours to the Regiment by Lady Saltoun. Among the guests were Provost Blaikie, Town Clerk John Angus and many other prominent citizens to the number of two hundred — a fact hilariously exploited by the defence advocates at the trial.

Strongly criticising the prosecution, the *Aberdeen Herald* was careful to excuse Superintendent Watson from involvement in the proceedings and commented: 'There is not in the City a more zealous and upright servant than Mr Watson, yet through this abominable Act and some of its sour-faced abettors amongst the Police Commissioners, he was placed in a most humiliating position.'

Cholera again! That was the alarming news which hit Aberdonians in the last week of August 1854. Many of the citizens still remembered the epidemic of 1832, in which one hundred and five people had died and they feared even a more serious outbreak. Poor drainage, lack of sanitation and too many closely built, dilapidated and over-crowded houses contributed to the spread of the disease.

The first cases were reported on Thursday, 24 August; the victims being James Davidson and his daughter, from Red Lion Court, Broad Street. They were part of a family of five, all of whom slept in one bedroom measuring seven feet by seven.

By the end of the first month, there had been sixty-two cases, thirty-eight of them proving fatal. The epidemic raged for three months, by which time the death toll had risen to one hundred and seventy-eight including many children. The majority came from dirty, unwholesome localities and many of the adults had been of intemperate habits. The outbreak struck many parts of the country and in London, in one week alone, over two thousand five hundred people perished.

During the epidemic in Aberdeen, the authorities conducted a vigorous advertising campaign to induce citizens to regulate their diet carefully and to be temperate and clean in their habits. Superintendent Watson's men assisted by reporting obvious health hazards, distributing disinfectants and taking any further action recommended by Dr Ogston.

In June 1850, the Police Commissioners and the Aberdeen Harbour Commissioners agreed in principle to merge their police forces; the latter then controlling a separate force of a few watchmen and a Superintendent. However, it was not until September 1854, that a formal merger proposal was placed before the Police Commissioners and Superintendent Watson asked to report on the proposition. He reported favourably and recommended three men for day duty at the Harbour, and four as night-watchmen, the Harbour Superintendent being absorbed into the city's Night-Watch force as a Sergeant. The recommendations were approved and the Harbour Commissioners agreed to make full financial provision for men doing duty in the Harbour area.

This merger brought to the ranks of the city's police, a distinguished poet, a William Anderson, whose first edition of *Rhymes, Reveries and Reminiscences* was published in 1851. Anderson, who had been born in the Green in 1802, was a coppersmith and factory-worker before joining the Harbour Police in 1849, at the age of forty-seven. He possessed genuine poetic inspiration, his best known work, 'Jean Findlater's Loun' giving a vivid account of the escapades of a mischief-maker of the day. Many of his poems were based on real life characters encountered during his police work — the 'wastrel gangrel bodies', as he called them. Anderson attained the rank of Lieutenant, by the time of his death in 1867.

Although Sheriff Watson was still active in the field of juvenile delinquency, his efforts had been adversely affected in recent years. The Presbyterian ladies of the Established and Free Churches, who ran the Female Industrial School in Long Acre, decided to part company and, at the break-up, the majority of the girls followed the Free Church ladies. They set up a similar establishment — 'Sheriff Watson's School' — in Skene Street.

The generosity of Dr George Watt was a great stimulant to the Sheriff, whose health was beginning to decline. Dr Watt's only son had died of cholera and he resolved to use his wealth for the benefit of the community. He had already financed the House of Refuge and now bought the lands of Oldmill, on the western outskirts of the town, for the erection of a larger establishment for the treatment of young offenders. In September 1854, it was decided that a Reformatory and Industrial School, as an auxiliary to the existing ones, be built at Oldmill.

Dunlop's Reformatory School Act, 1855, the name by which the Reformatory and Industrial School Act of that year was known, empowered Magistrates to send juvenile delinquents to approved Industrial Schools and the Aberdeen establishments were, of course, included. This development expedited the Oldmill project which was completed in 1856.

One of its first inmates was a young character named Gammie. The exploits of Lord Raglan and his men in the Crimean War had fired Gammie's imagination and along with other high spirited youngsters, he frequently staged 'Russians *v.* Allies' battles on the Links. The Broad Hill represented the heights of Balaclava and Gammie assumed the role of Lord Raglan, the gallant leader of the British Forces. During one assault on the Russian trenches, 'Lord Raglan' displayed so much vigour that he was apprehended on a charge of Breach of the Peace and fined ten shillings, with an alternative of ten days' imprisonment.

There was public outcry at the sentence. One citizen paid the fine and Mr William McCombie of the *Aberdeen Free Press* took Gammie into his own home and sent him to school. However, Gammie's seemingly irrepressible conduct had to be curbed. He was sent to the Oldmill Reformatory as a voluntary pupil and acquitted himself well. He eventually went to sea and rose to become an officer of a liner.

On 12 July 1856, Superintendent Watson was authorised by the Watch Committee to employ two men in plain clothes as 'Criminal Officers'. From this humble beginning, stemmed the present-day Criminal Investigation Department. The appointments were for six months in the first instance, but the experiment was continued and by the end of a year the appointments were confirmed. However, only one Criminal Officer was permitted to wear plain clothes. He received an allowance in lieu of uniform. In reaching their decision regarding the appointment of Criminal Officers, the Watch Committee paid due regard to the theft statistics for the ten years ending in 1855. The figures revealed that in only a quarter of the eleven and a half thousand cases reported had the thieves been detected.

The suppression of vice was given a high degree of priority by the Commissioners towards the end of 1857. It was estimated that there were about four hundred prostitutes and many brothels in the city, but the authorities and the police were handicapped by the lack of statutory power to deal adequately with the situation. Nevertheless, Superintendent Watson was directed to enforce rigorously his limited powers under the Aberdeen Police Act, 1818 and the Public House Regulation Act of 1854. In consequence of the directive and during the next few weeks, twenty-five women were reported for 'annoying persons in the streets' and two unlicensed eating houses — one in the Guestrow and the other in Upperkirkgate — were closed for being 'disorderly houses'. 'Harry the nests and the craws will flie awa' was the dictum applied to the situation by Police Commissioner Calder.

Thursday, 15 October 1857, was a day of great jubilation. A record crowd thronged King Street and Union Street for the visit of Queen

Victoria, Prince Albert and members of the Royal Family, who had been on a visit to Haddo House, the home of The Premier Earl of Aberdeen. They gave Her Majesty a welcome never before equalled in the city. The Queen and The Prince Consort had won a cherished place in the hearts of North-East people by their purchase of Balmoral Castle and by their frequent visits to the area. The Queen's remark on this occasion, 'It affords me great gratification to be once more in my City of Aberdeen,' was deeply appreciated by the citizens. From the police standpoint, Superintendent Watson and his men had no un-toward incidents to report.

The passing of the Counties and Burghs Police (Scotland) Act in 1857 was to have a far-reaching effect on the organisation and structure of the service in Scotland. The initial reaction of the independent minded Police Commissioners of Aberdeen was one of resentment.

The legislation was introduced to Parliament by The Lord Advocate and in June 1857, copies of the Bill were circulated to local authorities. The main provisions were these: Burgh Police Forces were to be merged with those of the Counties; a Government Inspector of Constabulary was to be appointed; and a quarter of the cost of police pay and clothing was to be paid by the Government, subject to the grant of a 'Certificate of Efficiency' by the Secretary of State, founded on the Inspector's report.

'Highly Objectionable!' was the city Commissioners' reaction to the proposal that the Force should be merged with that of Aberdeen-shire, but as the provision was to be at the discretion of local authorities, there was no need to petition against it. With regard to the other proposals, the Commissioners were prepared, at this stage, to accept in principle, the appointment of an Inspector of Constabulary and the suggestion that the Government should meet their quota for the Force's pay and allowance for clothing.

The first man to hold the office of H.M. Inspector of Constabulary in Scotland was Colonel John Kinloch of Logie, Kirriemuir, Angus. Born in 1807, Colonel Kinloch had pursued a distinguished military career in the 2nd Life Guards and 68th Light Infantry Regiments and had seen active service in the Crimean War.

In April 1858, he wrote to The Lord Provost seeking information about the size, organisation, pay and conditions of the city's police force. Although he was supplied with the necessary information, the following motion was put forward by Commissioner Ness and subsequently passed unanimously by the Police Board.

'That the Commissioners of Police would very much regret to see the City of Aberdeen placed under the "Counties and Burgh Police (Scotland) Act" passed last year and they therefore would decline to take advantage of the offer to have 25% of the Police expenses from the consolidated fund, as they consider the whole centralising system now seeking to be introduced, coupled with the grants from the State Treasury, to be a system fraught with danger to the liberties of the people.'

In March 1859, the Commissioners were advised that Colonel Kinloch proposed to inspect the Force on 5 April. Accordingly, they resolved that, without in the least compromising their former opinions and resolutions, they would give him an opportunity of conferring with the Board.

At this conference, Colonel Kinloch pointed out that every county and every burgh in Scotland, without exception, came within the scope of the Act, but his inspection alone did not commit the Commissioners to accept the grant which would be paid only when, following his report, a 'Certificate of Efficiency' was issued by the Secretary of State. The Colonel expressed dissatisfaction with much of what he had seen during the inspection but reserved final judgement on the Force's general state of efficiency, until he had given careful consideration to all the circumstances and made his report to the Home Secretary.

The outcome was inevitable. In June 1859, official intimation was received from Whitehall, London, that the Secretary of State did not feel justified 'in granting the certificate required by the Act to authorise the Lords Commissioners of the Treasury to pay any sum towards the maintenance of the Police'. A copy of Colonel Kinloch's report accompanied the letter and the Commissioners bitterly resented its content.

City of Aberdeen

'This ancient City (the capital of the great County of that name) has greatly increased in population since 1851 and has now 80,000 inhabitants.

'The Police Commissioners of the City are the only public officers in Scotland who questioned my authority to inspect and report upon the state of efficiency and discipline of their Police. Notwithstanding the explanation of their chief Magistrate, the Lord Provost, they appeared to consider that I was not authorised to do so, until they had formally decided, what they termed "to adopt the Act".'

'When I first proposed to inspect the Aberdeen force on 29th June, 1858, I received the following telegraphic despatch:

Provost Webster, of Aberdeen. To Colonel Kinloch of Logie:

"Do not trouble yourself to visit Aberdeen at present with reference to the City Police force. The Commissioners resolved in my absence not to place themselves under government inspection."

'I, however, went on to Aberdeen and informed the Lord Provost that my inspection was authorised by the 65 Section of the Act, 20 & 21 Vic. C. 72 and that I had the honour to hold H.M. Commission under that Act.

'The Lord Provost very kindly assured me that his own opinion agreed with mine, but stated that the Police Commissioners were of a different opinion on the subject.

'I waited until the Police Year had expired, when I again intimated to the Lord Provost (on 26th March '59) my intentions of inspecting the City of Aberdeen Police, previous to reporting on it to the Home Secretary.

'The Commissioners of Police, at a meeting on the 1st April, 1859, resolved as follows: "The Board having heard Col. Kinloch's official communication of 26th ult. resolved that, as his proposed inspection of the force is a matter entirely distinct from any further questions arising on his report, it is, in their opinion, right and courteous for them, without in the least compromising their former opinions and resolutions, to give him an opportunity of conferring with the Board while he is officially in Aberdeen, and resolve to intimate to him accordingly.".'

On arriving in Aberdeen, I met the Lord Provost, Magistrates and Police Commissioners, and on my assuring them that my inspecting their Police force would neither lead to any interference with them and the Act under which they at present maintained their Police establishment, nor oblige them to accept of the public allowance, as authorised by the 66th Section of the New Statute, even if reported as being in a state of efficiency as to numbers and discipline, they at once accompanied me during my inspection of the men and requested me to return to the Boardroom and state my opinion of their force, and to inform them if there was anything I would suggest to improve their efficiency. I told them plainly, I had no difficulty in saying that I did not consider they were at present efficient in organisation or discipline and that these points should be attended to first, before taking up the question of numbers, which I was not yet prepared to report on, but which would be an after consideration.

'For this great and important City with 80,000 inhabitants and a Police force of about 80 men, there is only one Police Officer — the Superintendent — (with no assistant of any kind) and only one Sergeant by day and another by night.'

'The Constables are divided in the old fashioned way into "Day Constables" and "Night-Watchmen"; the latter being so far considered of an inferior class that they have less pay and are not thought worthy of putting into uniform like the Day Constables, being provided only with a great-coat, a broad flat bonnet and a big stick!

'Such a staff of Officers and Sergeants is evidently too small. There is hardly a burgh in Scotland with half-a-dozen men, that is not better organised.

'When the Superintendent is absent, either from illness or on public duty elsewhere, the whole force is under the day or night Sergeant. The pay of all ranks, and particularly of the Night-Watchmen, is not sufficient to attract into the Service the sort of men that are required, being from two shillings to five shillings per week less than the wages of the Constables in their own County Constabulary and other Police forces. The best men seldom remain long, for they can easily better themselves, almost anywhere else.

'The very fact of not giving the night men the same uniform as the day men, lowers them both in their own opinion and that of the public, and there is too little prospect of promotion to induce good men to remain in the force, when they do enter.

'The force requires the addition of at least one Inspector or Lieutenant, if not two; and three or four Sergeants by day and the same by night; and the formation of the Constables into three classes as is usual in other Town & County Police forces, with a rise of pay to all; as it is at present below the usual average.

'The Constables are allowed, what I consider to be improper, to carry a thick stick or cudgel instead of a baton, the acknowledged and legal symbol of a Constable's office.

'The office for transacting the Police business is dark, dirty and gloomy; the room of the Superintendent very small, close and damp; altogether inferior office accommodation to many small country Towns and Burghs.

'The cells are very cold, the windows being unglazed; inferior to any Prisons of the present day, and in my opinion not fit for the confinement of prisoners who are only taken up by the Police on suspicion, or for drunkenness, and who are not yet convicted of any crime, or committed by a warrant from a Magistrate to be imprisoned.

'Altogether, I consider this force to be behind the age, inefficient in organisation and discipline and to require a thorough reform.

'I beg to acknowledge the courteous manner in which I was received by the Lord Provost, and Police Commissioners and the way in which they received the suggestions and recommendations I considered my duty to propose.'

To say the Commissioners resented the report would be an understatement! The report was variously described as 'unjust and injurious', 'untrue' and 'bosh!' No blame was attached to Superintendent Watson. They knew that the criticism was directed at them and none other. Indeed, certain improvements recommended by the Superintendent within recent months, had been rejected as 'too extensive to be substantiated'.

They countered Colonel Kinloch's criticism regarding the lack of a Lieutenant, Inspectors and Sergeants, by claiming that the two Sergeants were in effect Lieutenants, and the 'patroles' the equivalent of Sergeants. They paid lower rates of pay because in Aberdeen wages were generally lower; the city was healthy to live in; rents and provisions were cheap; and the population was of 'comparative good order and quietness'.

They refused to accept the Colonel's disparaging remarks about the division of the Force into The Day Patrole and Night-Watch; in particular his inference that the latter was inferior. They asserted the Night-Watchmen were paid less because their duties were easier; wore greatcoats and bonnets instead of uniform, because such garb was better suited to the weather; and carried sticks instead of batons for the purpose of extinguishing street lamps.

They agreed, however, that the Watch-house accommodation was unsuitable, but did not concur in the Colonel's remarks about the cells. One Commissioner remarked, 'The police cells may not be attractive, but they are clean and safe, and should the unglazed windows deter any tenants, so much the better'.

But the anticipation of monetary assistance from the Government turned the scales. The Commissioners realised that improvements would have to be made and entered into correspondence with Colonel Kinloch as to what changes would be necessary before a Government grant would be paid. Colonel Kinloch recommended that the men of The Day Patrole and Night-Watch be re-classified as 'Police Constables' (First, Second and Third Class) and be dressed uniformly. Moreover the complement of the Force should be raised to one Superintendent, two Lieutenants, seven Sergeants, two Detectives and seventy-four Constables — a total of eight-six.

On the question of remuneration Colonel Kinloch stressed that men of good character, intelligence and education were required for the service and wages must be commensurate with those abilities — not that of 'mere ordinary labourers'. He recommended:

Superintendent	£200 per annum
First Lieutenant	£85
Second Lieutenant	£75
Sergeants (3)	23s. per week
Sergeants (4)	21s.
Detectives (2)	24s.
24 Constables (First Class)	19s.
25 Constables (Second Class)	17s. 6d.
25 Constables (Third Class)	16s.

Moreover, blue uniforms, including frock coats, greatcoats, waterproof capes and hats were suggested.

The Commissioners realised only too well that the recommendations would involve a substantial increase in expenditure and accordingly met on 12 April 1860, to examine the cost. However, a pleasant surprise was in store for them. The new proposals would involve an additional outlay of one thousand and sixty-one pounds, but the Government grant to which they would be entitled would provide an income of one thousand, one hundred and fifty-two pounds — a saving of ninety-one pounds! A motion to adopt the new proposals was forthwith carried. Colonel Kinloch was well satisfied and the men delighted!

Superintendent Watson reorganised the Force in accordance with the recommendations. He did so in his usual quick and efficient manner. But the task was not easy and profound regret was felt by the Community when he died suddenly, barely a year later, on 24 April 1861.

E

Chapter Eight

1861–68

The new rank structure introduced at Colonel Kinloch's insistence meant that, on the death of Superintendent Watson, First Lieutenant James Duthie automatically took control of the Force until a successor was appointed. The post was advertised at a salary of two hundred and ten pounds. Twenty-five applications were received, including that of Lieutenant Duthie, who was placed on the short leet along with Superintendent John Swanson from Edinburgh and George Ingram from Paisley. The candidates were interviewed on 5 August 1861, and Duthie was selected.

The new Superintendent, though efficient, appears to have been a dour and determined individual, certainly not a colourful figure like 'Big Bob', a member of the Force at this time. 'Big Bob' — Robert Murray Barnett — was described by William Carnie in his *Reporting Reminiscences* as 'a man of ponderous rotundity and over twenty stone in weight'. He was a native of Auchterarder, Perthshire, and had been cattle-herd, collier, labourer, strolling-player and clerk, before joining the Force as Watch-house clerk.

As a labourer, 'Big Bob' had worked at Rubislaw Quarry, where he was known as 'The Parson' from his habit of wearing a swallow tailed coat! His experience as a strolling-player together with his copper-plate handwriting had enabled him to obtain a clerical post at the Marischal Street Theatre, and from there he was appointed Watch-house clerk, a post which he held for seven years, until his death at the age of sixty. Warm-hearted and sincere, 'Big Bob' befriended many outcasts and criminals brought to the Watch-house; his parting remark to first offenders invariably being, 'Dinna come back here, or ye'll bring sorrow to your folk, and shame to yersel'.

It will be recalled that, in 1830, Superintendent Fyfe had introduced vehicular mobility to the Force by purchasing a handcart for the conveyance of drunk persons. It served the public nobly for thirty-three years and by 1863, Superintendent Duthie had to report to the Commissioners that the handcart 'was completely worn out and would not repair'. It was agreed that a new barrow, set on springs, should be provided at a cost not exceeding five pounds.

The new barrow, referred to by the lads as the 'New Times', was kept at the side door of the Watch-house in Huxter Row. On the slightest hint of its being required, these youngsters hastily gathered around it, ready, willing and able to provide the necessary motive power — and their assistance was much appreciated by the elderly members of the Force. Harnessed to the 'New Times', these youngsters skilfully negotiated narrow wynds and passages at breathtaking speeds. No doubt, many a drunk was shaken into sobriety or rendered unconscious by the time he arrived at the Watch-house door!

The Aberdeen Police and Waterworks Act, 1862, and the Public Houses (Amendment) Act, 1862, provided the police with greater powers to deal with the problem of vice and licentiousness. On 1 April 1864, Superintendent Duthie reported to the Commissioners on the effectiveness of the new legislation. His report contained some interesting statistics: the number of street walkers had dropped from four hundred to one hundred and eighty; the number of brothels from thirty-four to twenty-seven; sixty persons had been prosecuted for importuning in the streets; and twenty-five keepers of public houses, inns and refreshment houses had been reported for harbouring undesirables or for otherwise infringing the new legislation.

Colonel Kinloch's annual inspection of the Force generally took place in November or December and apart from his first visit, referred to in the previous chapter, he had been satisfied with the Force as a whole. He had, however, made several suggestions: a greater proportion of First Class Constables; the adoption of the City of London Police uniform with helmet; and the provision of housing to a proportion of the men. The only suggestion to be adopted immediately was to clothe the men in the uniform recommended, but with a hat instead of the proposed helmet. No action was taken on the other recommendations.

Towards the end of the year, the brutal murder of fifty-two-year old Mrs Anne Forbes, wife of William Forbes, Shoemaker, Virginia Street, attracted much public attention. Between two and three o'clock on the afternoon of Saturday, 3 December 1864, Mrs Forbes was found dying in the woods at Thainston, near Inverurie. She had sustained a depressed fracture at the back of her skull consistent with a heavy blow from an axe.

The County Constabulary investigated and sixty-two-year old George Stephen, Wood Merchant, Port Elphinstone, was arrested.

Enquiries had established that Stephen and Mrs Forbes had been associating for several years, and had frequently met near to the scene of the murder, Mrs Forbes walking there from Aberdeen.

On the day of the murder, one witness had seen the couple enter the plantation together, Stephen carrying an axe, while another had seen him coming from the direction of the wood alone — still carrying this axe.

When arrested, Stephen denied all knowledge of the crime, but at his trial at the spring sitting of the High Court, in 1864, he surprised everyone, including his Counsel, by pleading guilty. His Counsel, however, submitted that the prisoner was in a state of mind that made him incapable of pleading. Nevertheless, the jury found Stephen guilty of the murder and he was sentenced to be hanged on 17 May 1864. Petitions for clemency were organised on his behalf, and on 13 May, the Lord Provost received intimation from the Secretary of State that Stephen had been reprieved and was to be detained during Her Majesty's pleasure in Perth Prison Asylum. When so informed, Stephen nonchalantly remarked, 'Jist a whilie langer to live'.

Cholera once again made its unwelcome appearance in August 1866, and continued till the following January. However, on this occasion, the authorities were much better organised. Dr Ogston headed a team of four doctors and several senior medical students who conducted house-to-house visitations. All 'nuisances' or health hazards were recorded at the Watch-house and remedial action taken daily. A Sergeant was appointed to the temporary post of 'Inspector of Nuisances' to supervise clearance work and in particular to deal with the problem of overcrowding. The House of Refuge was used for the temporary accommodation of displaced persons. A Sergeant was put in charge of the removal of patients to hospital and two Constables were engaged full-time for this duty. In general, members of the public shunned the victims and one cab owner actually declined to provide a horse and cab for the removal of patients because his 'men refuse to have anything to do with it'. He offered, however, to sell a cab for the purpose to the Board — a bargain at twelve pounds!

Press advertisements and handbills informed the public how they could help combat the disease. They were asked to limewash all courts and passages; to ensure that drains were trapped; to stop throwing slops into ash-bins; and to treat obnoxious smells with disinfectant obtained free at the Watch-house.

By 17 January 1867, the epidemic was over, but not before it had claimed sixty-five victims. The authorities maintained that the number of deaths would have been far greater had it not been for the precautions taken, a justifiable claim as this outbreak of cholera was the city's last.

Sheriff Watson retired in 1866, having given thirty-six years invaluable service to the community. The Industrial School idea which he had pioneered in Aberdeen had been adopted in many cities and towns throughout the country. The Society of Advocates recorded a highly appreciated tribute to his work, part of which read,

'We feel that you are not only an upright and impartial judge, but also a kind and warm-hearted man, and we cannot close this address without adverting in a few words to the very eminent position which you have acquired for yourself by the practical application of your experience in criminal jurisprudence to the prevention and diminution of crime. As the originator and founder of that now national institution — the industrial schools — you have earned for yourself, as a benefactor to your country and your race, a reputation of which you have just cause to be proud, and we believe, although it is not generally known, that the reformatories for juvenile offenders are also the off-spring of your humane and active mind.'

A project which was to bring tremendous benefit to the citizens of Aberdeen was completed in October 1866. It was the River Dee Water Supply scheme at Cairnton, near Banchory, constructed at a cost of one hundred and twenty-three thousand pounds and designed to supply the city with five million gallons of water daily.

Queen Victoria recognised the supreme importance of the project by presiding at the opening on Tuesday, 16 October 1866, and in reply to an address by The Lord Provost, Her Majesty made this reply to the people of Bon Accord.

'I thank you for your dutiful address and am very sensible of this fresh mark of the loyal attachment of my neighbours, the people of Aberdeen.

'I have felt that, at a time when the attention of the country has been so anxiously directed to the state of the public health, it was right that I should make an exertion to testify my sense of importance of a work so well calculated as this to promote the health and comfort of your ancient city.'

Ninety-two policemen were on duty at the opening, sixty from Aberdeen City Police, twenty from Aberdeenshire Constabulary and twelve from Kincardineshire.

A year later, Deeside again became a centre of intense police activity. Well grounded reports had been received about a possible Fenian attack on the Queen at Balmoral. Major John Ross of the County Constabulary took command of a large body of police, including senior detectives from Scotland Yard, who were sent to the area. Also drafted in for security purposes, were men of the 78th and 93rd Highlanders. Strict security precautions were maintained for several weeks. Fortunately nothing occurred.

An event of some importance was to affect the Force in July 1867 — the Watch-house at No. 9 Huxter Row had to be vacated. The property was scheduled for demolition along with the remainder of the historic street to make way for the now familiar Municipal Buildings in Castle Street. Also displaced by the reconstruction work was the Police Court. Both were removed to the old Record Office, then situated in Castle Street at Justice Street. The building, which had been erected in 1779, was in poor shape and required extensive renovation to make it habitable. However, by September, the cell accommodation proved to be inadequate and to supplement it, an adjoining house was acquired at an annual rent of five pounds. Part of this was rented to 'a married constable with no children' — at three shillings a week — on condition he boarded three or four unmarried men, to be 'easily within the Superintendent's call'. This was the first married accommodation to be provided for Police in Aberdeen, and the Commissioners hoped that the arrangement would satisfy Colonel Kinloch, who, at each annual inspection, had impressed upon them the desirability of providing such accommodation. However on the Colonel's next visit, he stressed the need for even more housing not only in the Castle Street area, but also in other districts.

During 1867 and 1868, it was decided to implement more of the Colonel's recommendations. City of London style police helmets with leather binding and bronze ventilating crests were to be supplied and fitted with badges displaying the City Arms. Refinements were to be made on the uniforms: the Lieutenants' frock coats were to be braided and the Sergeants' coats adorned with gold embroidered collars and gold lace chevrons. The night-Constables were to be provided with whistles and the much criticised staffs or cudgels were to be withdrawn.

In June 1867, one of the most horrifying murders of the time shocked the citizens. The victim was a fifty-nine-year-old widow named Craig, who lived with her son John, a twenty-four-year-old clerk, in a flat at 7½ Canal Street.

During the afternoon of Tuesday, 25 June, their neighbours became suspicious when they realised none of them had seen Mrs Craig or her son since the previous Friday and their parrots and ducks had not been fed during that time. The flat was locked, but the neighbours succeeded in opening a window and a young servant girl climbed in. In the living room, she saw a hand protruding from bed-clothes on a couch. She touched it, then recoiled in horror. The police were called and the bed-clothes removed. Mrs Craig's dead body presented a horrible sight. Her head had obviously been battered with a blood-clotted hammer found on the floor nearby. Medical experts estimated that Mrs Craig had died during the night of Friday, 21st.

It was known Mrs Craig had often quarrelled with her son John and he had often used violence towards her. Consequently he was suspected of the murder. Within a few hours of the discovery of his mother's body, he was found helplessly drunk in a public-house in Justice Street. It was Thursday morning before he recovered sufficiently to make any statement and when he did, he denied having murdered his mother. He claimed he had last seen her alive on Friday, 21 June and he believed she had gone south the next day. He also maintained he had not returned to the house since the Friday.

In actual fact at noon on Saturday, 22 June the police had found John Craig drunk in Church Street, and had detained him in the Watch-house till Sunday morning. His subsequent movements to the time of his arrest on Tuesday had not been established.

However, on Wednesday, 30 October 1867, Craig stood trial for the murder of his mother at the High Court of Justiciary in Edinburgh. He pleaded 'Not Guilty'. As the case against Craig was based principally on circumstantial evidence, it was no surprise when the jury returned the verdict of 'Not Proven'.

Like the two previous holders of the office, Superintendent Duthie died in harness. In August 1868, he became ill and died the following month, on 21 September. The Commissioners appear to have made no comment on his death, other than to agree to pay his widow a gratuity equivalent to three months' of her husband's salary and to appoint First Lieutenant John Smith as *interim* Superintendent.

Chapter Nine

1868-79

For Superintendent John Swanson, Edinburgh, it was second time lucky, for in 1861, when Duthie had been appointed, he had been one of the unsuccessful candidates. This time the Commissioners selected Swanson from the twenty-four applicants. However, his selection was not unanimous, for Lieutenants John Smith, Aberdeen, Robert Adamson, Forfarshire and Archibald Sinclair, Glasgow, also found support. From Lieutenant Smith's printed application — now in the possession of his great grandson — it is obvious that canvassing was quite in order, for it contains written testimonials from several serving Magistrates and other leading citizens including a salmon fisher!

In this appointment a procedural change had to be met. The Aberdeen Police and Waterworks Act, 1862, had laid down that the Sheriff of the county had to concur in the appointment, and in the event of disagreement, the Lord Advocate would make the final decision. Fortunately, there was no disagreement and Superintendent Swanson took up duty on 1 December 1868, at a salary of two hundred and fifty pounds.

One of Swanson's first tasks was to smarten up the appearance of his men. He recommended better supervision; a reduction in working hours; better organised tours of duty and the appointment of a drill instructor.

To provide better supervision, he requested the Commissioner's approval for the return to regular police duty, as day-Inspector, of Sergeant James Milne, then engaged in the collection of rates; and for the upgrading of the principal night-Sergeant to the rank of Inspector. He also proposed to reduce the Constables' hours of duty by one and a half hours daily, so that the day-men worked ten and a quarter hours and the night-men, nine and a quarter hours. In addition, it was his intention to arrange the men's tours of duty into shifts which would provide a twenty-four hour service to the public, and make provision for the relief of half the night-Constables at three o'clock on Sunday mornings, thus enabling them to attend Divine Service.

The Superintendent believed that military drill was essential to good bearing and turn-out and suggested the Commissioners appoint one of the Constables, an ex-Army man, to the post of drill instructor, at an appropriate fee.

Most of the Superintendent's proposals were adopted, but they turned down the request for Sergeant Milne to return to regular duty. He was to remain in his capacity as rate-collector.

This rate-collecting duty by the police is not so extraordinary as it might appear, when it is recalled that prior to the year 1871 both the Commissioners of Police and the Town Council had powers to levy rates; indeed, the greater part of the city's finances was raised through 'The Police Rate'.

In February 1869, Colonel Kinloch carried out his Annual Inspection of the Force. He approved of the re-organised duties, but pointed out that the men's pay was less than in smaller towns such as Montrose, Arbroath and Dundee. He recommended, too, that a more rapid system of promotion should be introduced, in particular the upgrading of Constables to the higher classes. He repeated these observations during his next visit in March 1870, when he discovered the Commissioners had done nothing to improve the situation.

Early examples of 'Mutual Aid' — the agreement among police chiefs to lend and borrow manpower — appear in minutes of this period. In September 1869, fifteen Constables were dispatched to Caithness for four days, for duty at polling stations; and the following year, fourteen Constables were sent to Kincardineshire on the occasion of the Aberdeen tradesmen's holiday. Of these fourteen, seven took duty at Stonehaven, four at Banchory and three at Torry — then in Kincardineshire. A century ago, Stonehaven, Banchory and Torry were the popular holiday centres of the majority of Aberdonians.

In February 1870, when the Harbour Commissioners expressed dissatisfaction with the policing of the Harbour and Quays, Swanson recommended that one Inspector and eight Constables should take duty there permanently, the Harbour Commissioners bearing the expense of their wages and clothing. This they agreed to do and the change took effect on 1 March of that year.

On 4 June 1870, the Force Headquarters removed from the Old Record Office in Castle Street to new premises in the reconstructed Municipal Buildings. The new police headquarters occupied that part of the present building overlooking Concert Court — now occupied by City Chamberlain's Department — the main public entrance being in Broad Street.

The Aberdeen Municipality Extension Act of 1871, came into force on 1 August of that year. It transferred to, and vested in the Town Council, the whole powers, duties, functions and authorities of every kind, formerly held by the Commissioners of Police under the Aberdeen Police and Waterworks Act, 1862, and other relevant statutes.

The first meeting of the Town Council for police business took place on 18 November 1871, when a 'Watching, Lighting and Fires Committee' was appointed. The members were Baillie Ross, *Convener*; Lord Provost Leslie; Baillie Esslemont and Messrs Findlay, Graham, Tough, Paterson and Able. The 'Watching' duties assigned to the Committee were: 'To consider and report on all matters regarding Constables, which the Council as a Council may be required to perform under any Local or General Act and to carry out any Orders or Bye-Laws; and to provide uniforms for the Watching Force.'

As its title implies, the Act also legislated for an extension of the city boundary and to facilitate the policing of the newly acquired area, Swanson recruited a further thirteen Constables. The new recruits began duty on 10 November 1871 — the Committee approving their appointment some days later!

Unlike their predecessors, the members of the newly constituted Watching, Lighting and Fires Committee took a sympathetic view of applications for more pay. On Christmas Day, 1871, they had before them a petition for an increase from members of the Force and listened to a submission on the subject by the Superintendent. Seasonal goodwill would appear to have triumphed, the Council being recommended to adopt new rates of pay — a small increase for a number of the men and the first in ten years.

The new scale of wages did not improve the basic wages of the First, Second and Third Class Constables, but it introduced a new grade of 'Merit Class' Constable at a higher rate of pay, and twenty men were so classified. The new rates were:

First Lieutenant	£95 per annum
Second Lieutenant	£80
2 Inspectors	27s. per week
4 Sergeants	24s.
3 Sergeants	22s.
2 Detectives	26s.
20 Constables (Merit Class)	20s.
30 Constables (First Class)	19s.
30 Constables (Second Class)	17s. 6d.
10 Constables (Third Class)	16s.

At a subsequent meeting in April 1872, the Committee recommended that the Superintendent's salary be increased to three hundred pounds, twenty-five pounds to be in respect of the duties as Sanitary Inspector and Inspector of Unwholesome Food, then undertaken by the Superintendent of Police.

In September, further increases of up to two shillings a week were approved for all ranks, raising the Third Class Constable's weekly rate to eighteen shillings. A year later, a similar increase raised the lowest rate to nineteen shillings and the salary of the First Lieutenant to one hundred and five pounds.

In 1872, Colonel Kinloch was succeeded as Her Majesty's Inspector of Constabulary for Scotland by the Honourable Charles Carnegie. Born in 1833, he was the third son of Sir James Carnegie, 5th Baronet, Kinnaird Castle, Forfarshire. Prior to his appointment as H.M. Inspector, he had held commissioned rank in the 23rd and 27th Regiments for five years, before being elected and returned as Member of Parliament for Forfarshire. As H.M. Inspector, he paid his first official visit to the Aberdeen Force, on 22 January 1873, and inspected the men on parade in the Volunteer Drill Hall, Woolmanhill. He was well satisfied with the inspection.

Lifeboat disasters are always distressing, but a particularly tragic one involving the Stonehaven lifeboat occurred at the entrance to Aberdeen Harbour during the afternoon of Friday, 27 February 1874. About two o'clock, the lifeboat was called to the aid of a small sailing vessel in distress — *The Grace Darling* — heading northwards in very rough seas. The lifeboat had a crew of twelve but only two were regular members, the others having refused to sail on account of the unusually rough seas.

The Aberdeen Harbour Authorities were advised by telegram 'Barque passed Stonehaven in distress; lifeboat in pursuit, look out'. About four o'clock *The Grace Darling* was sighted sailing northwards. No distress signals were displayed. However, a few minutes later the Stonehaven lifeboat attempted to enter Aberdeen Harbour. It successfully rounded the south-breakwater but, when opposite the north pier, was engulfed by a huge wave and capsized. The boat righted itself. Seven men clung to the boat, but five were thrown into the icy water. Huge waves then tossed the boat on to the rocks at the north side of the pier and the seven men managed to scramble to safety. The other five were washed out to sea. The Aberdeen lifeboat succeeded in rescuing two of them but one was found to be dead when taken ashore.

The Grace Darling was itself wrecked off Rattray Head, when only one member of the crew survived, out of fifteen.

The Aberdeen police reported on the circumstances to the Procurator-Fiscal and a Board of Trade enquiry was held. Eye-witnesses criticised the delay of the Aberdeen lifeboat in putting to sea, but the enquiry did not attach blame to anyone. A young doctor James Burr and a medical student by the name of Hanson were commended for their prompt and untiring efforts to save life.

A further disaster occurred later the same year, on Friday, 9 October. About eight o'clock that night a fire broke out at the East and West Parish Churches — 'The Toun's Kirk'. Thousands of people flocked to the scene. Officers and men of the 56th Brigade Depot and of the drill ship, H.M.S. *Clyde*, assisted police and firemen in fighting the blaze. However, despite all efforts, extensive damage was caused to the fabric of both churches and the historic lead spire was destroyed.

On 19 April 1875, members of the Force petitioned the Town Council to ask the Government to introduce a bill for Police Superannuation in Scotland. The petition was referred to the Watching, Lighting and Fires Committee on 21 June, but the members decided to take no action in the matter. At the same meeting, however, the Committee resolved to revise the establishment and wage scales to conform to Her Majesty's Inspector's report, which authorised one Superintendent, two Lieutenants, three Inspectors, nine Sergeants, four Detectives, eighty-seven Constables, one female Turnkey; and recommended a scale of wages which meant a rise of one or two shillings a week for most ranks. However, the burden on the rates for maintaining the police force was greatly relieved in that year, when the Government increased its contribution from a quarter to a half of the total cost.

Since his appointment as Her Majesty's Inspector of Constabulary, Mr Charles Carnegie had always reported favourably on the efficiency of the Force. On 7 October 1875, however, he wrote to the Lord Provost pointing out that night-Constables should not be required to extinguish street lamps and that if the practice continued he would not regard the officers so employed as efficient and reckonable in terms of the Government grant. The letter was treated with much merriment in the Council, but the task of extinguishing the lamps eventually passed to those who lit them — the lamplighters.

Wednesday, 5 April 1876, was a local holiday, a Fast Day. The weather was unusually fine and, as was the custom on holidays, many

Aberdonians crossed the River Dee to Torry. Of course, Victoria Bridge did not exist at the time and holidaymakers crossed the river by ferryboat plying between Ferry Place and Maitland's Quay. The boat was drawn across the river by a wire rope, fastened at each end and passing round the boat wheel.

About three o'clock in the afternoon, the ferryboat — with seventy-six passengers on board instead of the regulation thirty — got into difficulties in mid-stream. Grossly overloaded and with the hull only a few inches above water, the wire became so strained that the boat-wheel could not be moved. Several of the passengers panicked and the ferry shipped water. Then, in an effort to ease the strain on the rope, a well-meaning person at the Torry end slackened it to allow the boat to drift with the current. Unfortunately, the result of this action caused the boat to move swiftly downstream only to be pulled up with a jerk. The rope snapped and the ferryboat capsized.

Thirty-two people, including many children, perished, despite the gallant efforts of many rescuers, in particular salmon fishermen and pilots who laboured for hours in their cobbles.

The police naturally had been very much involved in the disaster: they had helped in the rescue operations; they had notified relatives; they had spent much time in trying to find out who had been on the boat — a time-consuming and virtually impossible task until all the bodies were recovered eight days later. But in the meantime anxious relatives of missing people had to be placated.

A Board of Trade Enquiry, presided over by Captain Harris, R.N., was held within a fortnight of the tragedy. The Enquiry censured not only the management of the ferryboat, but also the man-in-charge on the fateful day. He had permitted overcrowding then left the boat before it sailed, leaving his assistant in charge.

The Town Council launched an appeal in aid of the next-of-kin. Her Majesty The Queen, The Town Council and The Harbour Commissioners each donated fifty pounds, and eighty-one pounds was raised at a concert given by the Aberdeen Musical Association.

The building of a bridge over the River Dee in line with Market Street had often been discussed before the catastrophe; indeed, on the previous day, the City of Aberdeen Land Association had decided to donate four thousand pounds to the venture if the Town Council would co-operate. The latter had been reluctant to do so in previous years, fearing that Torry might develop into a rival community. However, 'The Torry Ferryboat Disaster' so incensed public feeling that the Victoria Bridge project was given the go-ahead and the bridge was opened five years later, in 1881. A fitting memorial to the victims of the disaster.

Further improvements in the working conditions of the members of the Force took place in 1877. The holiday arrangements which had been in force since 1870 — two days annually for Third Class Constables and four days for the remainder — were reviewed. It was decided that Third Class Constables would be entitled to four days annually and First and Second Class Constables to seven days. Any member guilty of misconduct, however, was to forfeit his entitlement for one year. Furthermore, Constables on leave were forbidden to take other employment. Uniforms too, had to be re-examined in the light of a letter from the Home Secretary in April 1878. This letter pointed out that before the Government paid the grant in respect of uniform, Her Majesty's Inspector had to be satisfied with its quality and cost. New uniforms were obtained and Mr Charles Carnegie expressed his approval during the Annual Inspection on 13 October 1878.

On 12 November 1879, Superintendent Swanson, whose state of health had been giving cause for concern for some time, tendered his resignation. It read:

'My Lord Provost and Gentlemen,

Owing to the present state of my health, I find that I cannot partake all the duties of my office in such a manner as I could wish. I therefore beg leave to tender my resignation as at a month from the 15th instant, having then completed 11 years in your service. As to any allowance that may be made in respect of such service, I place myself entirely in your hands. I may mention that I have 6 of a family living with and almost solely dependent upon me.

With sincere thanks for many past favours.

I am,
My Lord Provost and Gentlemen,
Your obedient servant,
(Signed) John Swanson,
Superintendent of City Police.'

A similar communication was sent by Mr Swanson to the Sheriff of Aberdeen and Kincardine.

The Council accepted Superintendent Swanson's resignation and granted him an allowance of thirty shillings a week for one year.

Chapter Ten

1880-1902

14 December 1879 was Superintendent Swanson's last day in office and First Lieutenant George Dey — popularly known as 'The Longest Dey' on account of his height — was appointed *interim* Superintendent.

The post of Superintendent was advertised at a salary of three hundred and fifty pounds and forty-three applications were received. A short leet of eight candidates was drawn up. On this occasion the Sheriff of Aberdeen and Kincardine, Sheriff Guthrie Smith, was consulted, his first choice being Superintendent Donald Sutherland, Paisley; his second, either Chief Constable Alexander McHardy, Sutherland or Superintendent Thomas Wyness, Inverness. The Town Council favoured Wyness, and with the Sheriff's concurrence, the Lord Provost appointed him to the office on 27 January 1880.

The son of a farmer, Thomas Wyness was born at Midmar, Aberdeenshire in 1837. He attended the local school until he was twelve, when his father's untimely death necessitated his leaving to take employment to help support the family. Despite his youth, he determined that his broken education would not be disadvantageous to his future and he devoted all his leisure hours to study.

He joined the Aberdeenshire Constabulary as a Constable in 1859 and served in various parts of the county. He was promoted to the rank of Sergeant in 1862, and three years later applied for and obtained the Superintendentship of Elgin Burgh Police. Here he established himself as an efficient Police Chief and Procurator-Fiscal. His reputation spread. In 1872 he was appointed Superintendent of Inverness and eight years later came to Aberdeen as successor to Superintendent Swanson. He was the city's first 'Chief Constable'.

Wyness was a man of strong personality. Consequently he was either much admired or greatly disliked. He showed such conviction in carrying out his policies that the baillies seldom if ever disagreed with him, a novel situation viewed by some citizens with grave concern. A poem, 'The New Dictator', published in *The Bon-Accord* of Saturday, 11 September 1880, illustrates the point.

> We're coming now to curious fates
> In Aberdeen, 'twould seem;
> That we are ruled by Magistrates
> Turns out to be a dream.
> Why at elections make a fizz?
> They're naught to me or you;
> Our ruler now a Bobby is —
> If half they say be true.

Members of the licensed trade were the first to feel the wind of change. Wyness had found that the administration of the licensing laws left much to be desired. He adopted a strict policy and took such firm action that he became known as 'The Terror of the Trade'. He cracked down heavily on back-shop drinking in licensed grocers' shops, brought about the abolition of that instrument of concealed drinking — the 'treacle cask' or 'treacle cistern' — and to ensure better supervision of public houses, he insisted on the removal of compartments and the introduction of open counters.

Following the publication of 'The New Dictator' there appeared a modest publication called 'A Prayer', a poem of forty stanzas, wherein the author requests the Almighty to gather into Heaven 'the six Temperance Baillies', as being 'far ower gweed for Bon Accord', and to hand over His duties to 'Tam Wyness — Nummer Saven'.

> Ye're sure ye hae nae vacant place
> For this chiel, Nummer Saven?
> Oh Lord, we tell ye tae yer face,
> HE MAUN GET INTAE HEAVEN!
> And there HE must be KING — alone
> An Autocratic Highness,
> Come doon yersel' frae Heaven's Throne,
> AN' HAN' THE REINS TAE WYNESS!

However, the 'Terror of the Trade' despite the outcries against his measures, the lampooning, the caricaturing and many personal affronts, went on his way unperturbed — the embodiment of the Wyness motto *He yt tholis overcumis*.

On 8 December 1880, Dr Francis Ogston, the Police Surgeon resigned his post. He had served in this capacity for fifty years; indeed as has already been mentioned, he was the first to hold this appointment. Despite his large practice and the holding of several University posts — including the Chair of Medical Jurisprudence — Dr Ogston also served the community in several other spheres, such as Medical Officer of Health under the Public Health Acts, Medical Attendant at

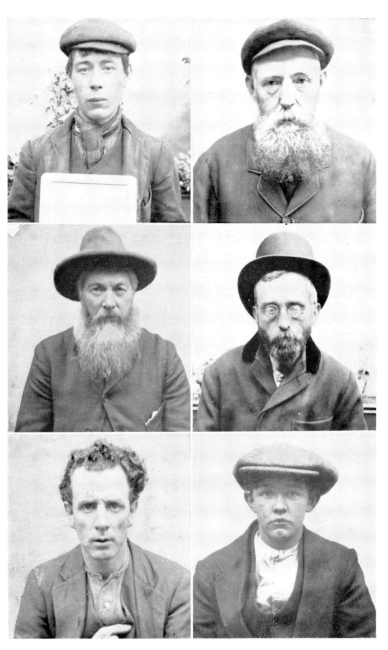

Male Prisoners
(late Nineteenth century)

Female Prisoners
(late Nineteenth century)

HEADQUARTERS
No. 9 Huxter Row 1820–67
Old Record Office, Castle Street—1867–70

HEADQUARTERS
Concert Court 1870–95
Lodge Walk 1895–1972

the Epidemic Hospital and at the Gas Works, and the Inspector under the Dairies, Cow-sheds and Milk-Shops Order, of 1879. For all these duties he received the annual salary of three hundred pounds.

Dr Francis Ogston was succeeded by a Dr William J. Simpson, M.D., C.M. of Dover, the Deputy Medical Officer of Health for East Kent. He was appointed to the post by thirteen votes to nine in the face of strong competition from Dr Francis Ogston, Junior, M.D., Aberdeen, the son of the previous holder of the office.

Chief Constable Wyness's appreciation of the value of education soon became evident. He provided the men with a reading room and a regular supply of newspapers and magazines, at an annual cost of nine pounds five shillings, and he obtained one hundred bound copies of the Police Acts for issue to individual members of the Force.

Improving the efficiency of his Force was always uppermost in the Chief Constable's mind and when in August 1881, the Town Council gave permission to the National Telephone Company Limited to establish a Telephone Exchange in the city, he was quick to realise the importance of the event. In June 1882, he advised his Committee on the desirability of connecting the Police Office with the newly established Telephone Exchange and expressed the view that telephone stations in the outskirts of the city would be an asset to police work. The Committee agreed, but as usual, in part only. Accordingly on 11 July 1882, they authorised the installation of a telephone in the Police Office, and two years later gave sanction for a phone in the Chief Constable's residence.

In 1881, Chief Constable Wyness obtained permission to recruit a further six constables by reason of the increase in population during the previous ten years, and in 1883, a further fourteen were recruited on account of the extension of the municipal boundary in that year.

The Honourable Charles Carnegie resigned as Her Majesty's Inspector of Constabulary for Scotland on 4 May 1884. He was succeeded by Captain David Monro, Chief Constable of the combined counties of Edinburgh and Linlithgow. Captain Monro had been a professional soldier. In 1857 at the age of eighteen, he had joined the Indian (Madras) Army as an Ensign and had served in India till 1873, rising to the rank of Captain. Ill-health had forced his retiral from the Army and on 1 January 1874 he had become Chief Constable of the Isle of Man Constabulary, a position which he held until May 1878. when he obtained the Chief Constableship of the Counties of Edinburgh and Linlithgow. In his new capacity as H.M. Inspector, Captain Monro paid his first official visit to Aberdeen on 18 August 1884 and expressed his satisfaction with the efficiency of the Force.

F

Horse Transport. Introduced by Wyness 1891

The following month, a new scale of pay, approved by the Home Secretary, was adopted by the Council. The maximum salary of a First Lieutenant was raised to two hundred pounds and that of a First Class Constable to one pound eight shillings weekly. At the same time, the Committee resolved to recommend that the salary of the Chief Constable should be increased from three hundred and fifty to four hundred pounds. In this connection, a petition — which members of the Committee agreed to disregard — was presented by a body of rate-payers and citizens urging the Council to delay consideration of the proposed increase until after the ensuing Municipal Election!

Captain Monro's second visit took place in July 1885. On this occasion he called for improvement in the cells and for enlarged office accommodation. In accordance with his advice, directions were given to remove the sloping board beds from the cells and to convert adjoining offices in the Municipal Buildings for use by the police department. However, the inadequacy of the accommodation became more marked year by year, as the range of police duties and commitments increased. Consequently it was not surprising that during successive visits Captain Monro passed some adverse comments on the subject. Ultimately, the following letter dated 29 December 1890 was received by the Town Clerk from the Secretary for Scotland.

'Sir,

Adverting to previous correspondence respecting the Aberdeen City Police Offices and Cells, I am directed by the Marquis of Lothian to state for the information of the Magistrates and Town Council that in his report on the results of the recent annual inspection of the City Police Force, Her Majesty's Inspector of Constabulary once more called attention to the fact that the Police Buildings, are inadequate, inferior and badly arranged.

In bringing this matter again under the notice of the City Authorities, I am to express the Secretary for Scotland's hope that it may have their early and serious consideration and to remind them that suitable police buildings are considered an essential part of an efficient and effective police establishment.

I am to add that in other respects, His Lordship was pleased to receive such a very favourable report on the state and efficiency of the Force.

I am, Sir

Your obedient servant,

(Signed) J.M. Dodds.'

If the Town Council were to be criticised for their failure to provide a suitable Police Headquarters, the same could not be said of the Prison Commissioners in respect of prisons. A new prison was in the course of construction at Craiginches, which was to replace the East Prison in Lodge Walk, the site of prisons in one form or another since 1394. Indeed, part of the Old Tolbooth prison, complete with condemned cell, erected between 1616 and 1629 remains to this day. It is also interesting to note that from 1809 to 1864 the city was particularly well served with prisons, possessing another rather forbidding example, the Bridewell or West Prison at the north end of Rose Street.

With the opening of Craiginches, the East Prison in Lodge Walk was closed on 9 June 1891, and the following month was offered for sale. With a new police headquarters in mind, the Town Council acted quickly and purchased the property from the Prison Commissioners, at the upset price of three thousand pounds. A new police headquarters, of which more will be written later, was opened there in 1895.

In the year, 1885, a bill was introduced into Parliament 'to make provision respecting the pensions, allowances and gratuities of police constables in Great Britain'. However, as the wheels of democracy turn slowly, legislation on the subject — The Police (Scotland) Act, 1890 — was not forthcoming until April 1891. Section I of the Statute enacted that policemen, who had completed twenty-five years' service and who were not less than fifty-five years of age, or sixty if holding a rank above that of Sergeant, were entitled to retire with a pension for life. Accordingly, on 16 April 1891, the undermentioned members of the Force intimated their intention to retire and they were awarded annual pensions as shown:

NAME	RANK	AGE	SERVICE	PENSION
James Milne	Lieutenant	66	41	£83: 9: 0
Smith Ewen	Inspector	65	42	£56: 1: 0
James Allardyce	Sergeant	60	34	£48:12: 8
Daniel Ross	Sergeant	55	33	£45:15: 0
James Anderson	Sergeant	66	40	£39:14: 4
Joseph Summers	Constable	61	31	£34:14: 3
William Walker	Constable	65	39	£39: 0: 8
James McPherson	Constable	60	26	£22:11: 5
Peter Watt	Constable	60	32	£32: 6: 9
Alexander Anderson	Constable	61	28	£23: 7: 3
James Cowie	Constable	59	28	£22:11:10

The Act also provided for the making of Regulations governing conditions of appointment of Constables and empowered Superintendents of Police to punish men guilty of misconduct or neglect of duty in one of the following ways: by the imposition of fines to an extent not exceeding two weeks' pay for each offence; by reduction in rank; by deduction of up to six months' service; or by dismissal.

In October 1891, approval was given to Chief Constable Wyness to augment the Force by one Inspector, two Sergeants and twenty Constables. The reason for this substantial increase was the incorporation into the city, of Old Aberdeen, Woodside and Torry, then independent communities.

Old Aberdeen had been a Burgh of Barony since 1498 and now had a population of about two thousand six hundred. It had its own Provost, Magistrates and Town Council, a self-elected body, who were also Commissioners of Police. For its supply of gas and water it had been almost entirely dependent upon the city.

Woodside had been a Police Burgh since 1868 under the General Police and Improvement (Scotland) Act, 1862. It had its own water supply but had also depended on the city for gas.

Neither of these burghs had a separate police force, both being policed by Aberdeenshire Constabulary.

The village of Torry in the parish of Nigg, Kincardineshire, had been a Burgh of Barony since 1494. It was now entirely dependent on the city for water and gas, but had been policed by Kincardineshire Constabulary.

The inhabitants of Old Aberdeen and Woodside had been generally in favour of their annexation by the city, but a poll of Torry ratepayers taken on 27 September 1890 revealed that only fifty-eight were in favour while two hundred and eighty-nine were against.

The increased area of the city presented the Chief Constable with the task of devising a system whereby his men could be regularly deployed in all districts without losing contact with Headquarters. He concluded that the solution lay in providing, at carefully selected sites throughout the city, police sub-stations linked by telephone to Headquarters. The Town Council agreed and in October 1891, it was decided to convert for the purpose the existing police stations in Woodside and Old Aberdeen and the Fire Engine Station at Causeway-end. It was also agreed to erect three teak buildings — similar to Glasgow Police sub-stations — one at the west end of Fonthill Road, one in Victoria Road at Sinclair Road with the third in Leadside Road at Northfield Place. All of them had cells, accommodation for fire-hose reels, and hand ambulances — recent acquisitions which resembled the traditional casualty stretchers but mounted on bicycle wheels.

The increased area also emphasised the need for greater mobility. In August 1891, the Chief Constable obtained authority to police the outlying districts by 'six men in pairs mounted on bicycles', and the following month was authorised to accept an offer by the Aberdeen District Tramways Company to supply nine-and-a-half-thousand tramway tickets yearly, for the sum of twelve pounds ten shillings. In December, he obtained permission to hire, at sixty pounds per annum, a horse and driver for the prison van, a horse for himself to ride, or a horse and dog-cart for him to drive.

In February 1892, the Watching Committee called upon the City Architect to report on the possibility of converting the East Prison in Lodge Walk to a new Police headquarters. In June, John Rust Jr., City Architect, submitted two schemes for the consideration of the Committee, both schemes to cost ten thousand pounds.

The first was a re-construction scheme. In plan the East Prison was a square. The architect suggested that one of the wings — the north wing — could be retained in its existing form to provide a block of cells, but the other wings would require to be doubled in width to provide the required accommodation.

The second scheme was to demolish the entire prison and erect a new building on the site. This was to consist of a main block, four flats high, extending along Lodge Walk, with two wings at right angles. The most northerly wing was to be a cell block, two floors in height and having accommodation for twenty-two male and eight female prisoners. A feature of the proposed new building was the provision of bedroom cubicles for thirty-five Constables. A further report recommended the inclusion of a gangway linking the Sheriff court-house and Municipal Buildings with the new Police Headquarters 'to allow agents to go from one court to another in a minute or so'.

The Committee recommended that the reconstruction of the existing prison building would not be satisfactory and that an entirely new Police Headquarters should be erected. The Council agreed and tenders were invited. The lowest was four and a half thousand pounds in excess of the estimate. The plans were re-examined and on 16 March 1893, it was decided, after hearing Chief Constable Wyness — the first occasion on which the designation Chief Constable was minuted — to depart from the proposal to provide sleeping accommodation for the Constables, thereby reducing the cost to ten thousand one hundred and eighty-seven pounds.

In June 1894, a gymnasium was added at a cost of two hundred pounds and it was agreed that the building would be wired and fitted for electricity for an extra one hundred and fifty pounds.

On 1 October 1895, the new Police Headquarters in Lodge Walk was opened and this is the building still in use. Commenting upon the event and the early development of the Force, the *Aberdeen Journal* of 28 September 1895 reported:

'A chapter of local history, not without interest, is the institution and growth of the police force, which is about to remove to its new and handsomely equipped headquarters in Lodge Walk. To moral philosophers of the school of Councillor James Gray, the need of such a body may be fraught with melancholy reflections. . . .'

Significant, therefore, is the following motion of 16 December 1895. 'That the Council decline to confirm the action of the Committee so far as it relates to the payment of an account amounting to £41:6:9d. incurred in connection with a luncheon on the occasion of the opening of the New Police Buildings on 1 October last. No authority for the expenditure having been obtained from the Council.' The motion was proposed by Councillor Alexander Wilkie and seconded by Councillor James Gray!

The following year, on the 30 September, 'The Jollity Theatre' was completely destroyed by fire. 'The Jollity' — now the site of 'The Palace' ballroom in Bridge Place — had originally been the home of Cooke's circus. With seating capacity for two thousand, many people felt that the exits were too restricted, but an evacuation exercise organised sometime previously by the Magistrates revealed that the theatre could be cleared in four minutes.

Fortunately, on the night of the fire, there were only five hundred patrons. About eight o'clock, when some of the scenery was being moved between acts, some flimsy articles came in contact with gas jets and ignited. The flames spread rapidly. The audience panicked and rushed the exits. In the press several fell and were trampled under foot. Unhappily, seven people died and twenty-six were injured.

On 28 January 1897, Sheriff Substitute Brown gave judgement in an action for damages raised at the instance of James Cameron of Woodside against Detectives Smith and Dey, for his alleged illegal apprehension. The Sheriff found the defenders Smith and Dey each liable to the pursuer in the sum of five guineas with expenses amounting to thirty pounds. The Chief Constable asked the Watching Committee to relieve Smith and Dey of the damages and expenses and the Committee agreed. Five Councillors dissented, including Councillors Gray

The Jollity Theatre Fire 1896

and Wilkie! The reasons for their dissent are of interest. The Town Council were not legally liable for the actions of police officers; the use of rates to pay damages and expenses would be improper; to make payment would be tantamount to condoning the offences; the officers concerned were experienced and acted in contravention of their Chief Constable's instructions; and it would create a precedent whereby other officers would expect similar protection — a situation which might encourage irresponsibility and endanger the liberty of the subject.

About this time a citizen's right to express himself freely was exercised in a rather unusual way by George Russel, Sculptor. Readers will recall the grim bearded face which, until a few years ago, adorned the corner stone of Russel's property in Ragg's lane, on the west side of Broad Street opposite Queen Street. It seemed Russel had a grievance against one of his neighbours, an ironmonger named Stephen, and to express his feelings he carved the head — a caricature but an excellent likeness of Stephen — and erected it in such a position that Stephen saw it each time he came out of his house. Obviously planning permission had not yet come to the city!

However, Russel did not feel the same animosity towards Constables and scavengers for even to this day each Constable and scavenger receives, on the anniversary of the sculptor's death, several shillings — the free income from his estate — which he bequeathed to 'the Constables of the police force and the ordinary scavengers' — with the proviso that, 'the officers of the police force and the foreman of the scavengers are not to participate . . . .'.

'The Nellfield Cemetery Scandals' of 1899 brought the city much notoriety.

Nellfield Cemetery in Great Western Road was owned by the Aberdeen Baker Incorporation. The first indication that all was not right was given in the month of May, when a civil action was brought against the Baker Incorporation alleging interference with a grave. Disclosures during the proceedings gave rise to deep public disquiet and a searching investigation followed. William Coutts, the Cemetery Superintendent, was eventually arrested and charged with seven crimes: six of violating sepulchres and one of perjury arising from the civil action.

Consequently, from 6 to 9 June, official excavations were carried out at the cemetery. The result of these investigations were quite revolting. A few feet below the surface of a pathway, the doubled up remains of a young woman and a middle aged man were found uncoffined. Several graves were then opened and ample evidence came to light of the most distressing practices: before the bodies had decayed the coffins had been removed and burned; bodies had been disinterred without the knowledge of relatives and buried elsewhere; unrelated bodies were found together; and old coffin lids, name plates and handles were found alongside recent interments.

Cemetery employees admitted interfering with graves, lifting coffins and removing bodies but said they acted on instructions from Coutts. The extent of their activities was made clear in their evidence. In some cases corpses were 'coupit' from the coffins into the graves with the lids being placed over the bodies and the coffins burned. In one instance a workman admitted 'trailing' bodies from one grave to another while another stated he had 'broken up' a body with a shovel.

The purpose of these revolting practices was not hard to seek — monetary gain. The removal of the coffins created more interment space which could be sold and it saved labour — for less earth had to be barrowed away than if the whole coffin had been interred.

The trial of William Coutts took place at the High Court of Justiciary which opened on 6 September 1899. A large crowd tried to get into the Court-house and Chief Constable Wyness took personal charge of the police arrangements. Lord McLaren presided. The prosecution was led by Mr James Fleming, Advocate-Depute and the accused's counsel was Mr J. Crabb Watt, Advocate, Edinburgh. The accused pleaded 'Not Guilty'.

After Lord McLaren had heard and repelled objections to the relevancy of the libel, evidence was led in support of the seven charges on the indictment. On the fourth and final day of the trial, counsel for the accused tendered pleas of guilty to two of the charges of violating sepulchres. The Advocate-Depute accepted the changed pleas on behalf of the Crown.

In his address to the jury Lord McLaren said:

'I hope that the exposure of the conduct of the interments in this cemetery, so revolting in its details and shocking to the natural feelings — not only of the relatives of those who are removed, but of many who fear that their dead might be treated in the same way — will prove an effective safeguard against the possibility of such practices continuing in any cemetery in Scotland.'

His Lordship then directed the jury to find Coutts guilty of the two charges of violation of sepulchres to which he had pleaded guilty and not guilty of the others. The jury complied.

In passing sentence, Lord McLaren said to Coutts,
'I take into account, in considering the punishment, that in the first place, it must be a substantial punishment in order to satisfy the ends of justice. It is not of the most severe character, because this is not a case of raising bodies for sale, that would be theft; neither was it done for the purpose of extorting money by working upon the feelings of relatives. It was a case of breach of trust to the relatives who paid for these interments. In such circumstances, your acts constituted, by the law of Scotland, a violation of sepulchres. I am also willing — very willing — to give what weight I can to the points so well submitted and brought out by your counsel that this is the first case in which it has been found necessary to take action against any cemetery officials for a series of desecrations. Though you must know that your conduct amounted to a moral offence, you may not have been fully aware of the criminal responsibility that resulted from your acts. In the circumstances, I feel warranted in limiting the sentence to a period of six months' imprisonment.'

In 1901, another serious crime occupied the attention of Chief Constable Wyness — 'The Park Street Murder'. A slaughterhouse butcher, James Harrow, murdered two of his fellow butchers in the 'Saltoun Arms' public house in Park Street, on the night of 9 January. One of the victims, William Tastard, died almost immediately from severe knife wounds while the other, David Ewing, died in hospital four days later. Harrow was found to be insane and was detained during His Majesty's pleasure.

Towards the end of the year, the Chief Constable's health began to deteriorate. In January 1902, he was granted prolonged sick leave and Mr William Anderson, who had been upgraded from Lieutenant to senior Superintendent and Deputy Chief Constable in March 1899, was instructed to take charge of the Force. However, the chief's health did not improve and Wyness died on 23 December 1902.

On 5 January 1903, the Town Council met and the minute of that date referring to the Chief Constable's death is a tribute in itself:
'It was with feelings of deep regret that the Lord Provost had to intimate to the Town Council the death of Mr Thomas Wyness, Chief Constable, which took place on 23rd of last month. By the death of Mr Wyness, the Magistrates and Council had lost the services of an old and esteemed official, who discharged his duties with conscientiousness, impartiality and independence. In the Police Force of which he was the head, he took the deepest personal interest and spared no effort to raise its standard and promote its

efficiency. Mr Wyness enjoyed the respect and esteem of all classes of the community who recognised and appreciated the earnestness and ability which characterised the performance of his difficult and responsible duties.'

Chief Constable Wyness left behind him a Force of men of above average intelligence and education, who had been well trained in professional subjects, first-aid, swimming and gymnastics. In April 1899, he had made provision for a mounted section by acquiring riding boots and saddlery and contracting for the hire of suitable horses whenever they were required. This proved invaluable in dealing with crowds such as on the occasion of the Students' Rectorial Election on 10 November 1899, when a large body of apprentices attempted to disrupt the students' procession at Queen's Cross, but were foiled by the timely intervention of the mounted section with Wyness in command.

As previously mentioned Wyness had also obtained a new head-quarters, and sub-stations at Woodside, Old Aberdeen, Causewayend, Fonthill, Torry, Northfield Place and Queen's Cross — the last mentioned having been built in October 1898. Moreover, within a year of his death he had prevailed upon the Town Council to purchase, at six hundred and fifty pounds, buildings at the north end of his headquarters in Lodge Walk to provide for its future expansion.

Chapter Eleven

1903-32

The Town Council and Sheriff Donald Crawford approved the appointment of Mr William Anderson, the Deputy Chief Constable to succeed Chief Constable Wyness. The appointment was made on 8 January 1903, and the salary fixed at four hundred and fifty pounds per annum.

Born in 1860, Anderson was the son of an Angus farmer. At the age of fifteen, he entered the office of the Forfarshire Procurator-Fiscal and remained there until 1890, when he joined the Police Force as a Constable. In doing so, he sacrificed a salary of one hundred and twenty pounds a year for a weekly wage of one pound four shillings and sixpence. However, his legal knowledge and administrative experience stood him in good stead and promotion was rapid. In nine years he rose to become senior Superintendent and Deputy Chief Constable.

Anderson took over an efficient force with a complement of one hundred and sixty-eight, comprising in addition to himself, two Superintendents, six Inspectors, eleven Sergeants, eight Detectives and one hundred and forty Constables. The numerical strength of the Force, however, did not completely satisfy the Secretary of State who had recommended the number be raised to one hundred and ninety-five. This was in keeping with the suggestion made by Chief Constable Wyness two years before. Anderson held the same opinion. A few weeks after his appointment the new Chief Constable drew to the attention of the Watching Committee, the fact that during 1902, six Constables had resigned to join other Forces. He feared if he could not improve the men's working conditions, Aberdeen would soon become 'a Training School for other Forces'.

The main grievance concerned hours of duty which in Aberdeen were longer than in any other large town. In order to alleviate this, Anderson obtained authority to appoint a further two Sergeants and ten Constables, which enabled him to give each man one day off duty every month. Previously men on day duty had been granted three hours off every third week and men on night duty two hours every second week!

In a further move to improve the morale of his men, Chief Constable Anderson cancelled the standing order which forbade policemen from taking meal-breaks inside police buildings. For example, the policemen on the Queen Street beat was permitted to heat his tea-flask in a pot of boiling water in the Muster Room but must resort to his recognised dining room to drink it — the doorway of the Banks of Ythan public house at the corner of Queen Street and Lodge Walk!

In April 1903, it was agreed to obtain new helmet badges. The existing badges, which had been in use since 1868, proved too large for the recently introduced summer-wear caps. Accordingly, it was decided to procure a badge which could be worn on either helmet or cap and one representing both the controlling authorities of the Force — the Town Council and the Government. The result was a smaller badge containing a modified version of the city's Armorial Bearings surmounted by the Imperial Crown. Initially, one hundred and eighty badges were supplied by the Aberdeen firm of Messrs George Jamieson and Son, Jewellers, at a cost of elevenpence each! They were cast in white metal and silver-plated. Still worn by members of the Force, this badge is the only local police badge in use in Scotland, the other forces having adopted the recognised badge of the Scottish Police Service.

In 1904, Captain Monro was succeeded as His Majesty's Inspector of Constabulary for Scotland by Major Sir Arthur George Ferguson, C.B.E., D.S.O., of Pitfour, Aberdeenshire. Born in 1862, Ferguson was educated at Eton, and, as a young man, was commissioned in the Rifle Brigade seeing active service in the South African War. Apart from the duration of the First World War, when he served with his Regiment as a Lieutenant-Colonel, Ferguson held the position of His Majesty's Inspector until 1927. He was awarded the C.B.E. in 1920 and knighted seven years later.

The official opening of the new Marischal College buildings by King Edward VII and Queen Alexandra on Thursday, 27 September 1906, presented Chief Constable Anderson with the greatest challenge of his career. To cope with the event, he employed eight hundred and seventy-eight policemen, seven hundred and five being seconded from other forces. 'A policemen's lot is not a happy one' might well have applied to this historic occasion. The policemen mustered at quarter to six in the morning, had their first meal at seven in the evening and were dismissed at midnight.

Commenting upon the event *The Evening Gazette* of 28 September 1906, reported:

'Deep satisfaction is today the dominant note in respect to the visit of the King and Queen to the city yesterday. The weather was perfect; military and Police arrangements were excellent; and the University and Civic functions had been carefully thought over and admirably prepared for.'

Referring particularly to the police, the same paper commented,

'Pleasure is being expressed at the notable success that attended all the ceremonies, for which the admirable police arrangements, supervised by Chief Constable Anderson, are largely due.'

October of the following year, 1907, saw the formation of the Aberdeen City Police Pipe Band with nine pipers and four drummers. Such was the interest and enthusiasm for the project that members of the Force had subscribed to a fund for the provision of instruments and uniforms. Consequently, no financial assistance was required from the Town Council.

For some time, Anderson had felt that specially distinguished conduct by members of his Force should be recognised in some tangible way and in July 1909, the Town Council agreed to provide silver medals for presentation to deserving officers.

The first award of the medal was made in August of that year to Constable William Ritchie who had specially distinguished himself in effecting the arrest of a burglar in Torry in the previous February. The incident occurred at the 'University Bar,' Sinclair Road, the public house now styled the 'Nineteenth Hole.' About four in the morning Ritchie had heard the sound of breaking glass at the bar. He went immediately and saw two men, one of whom dived through a window and escaped whilst the other threw a heavy object at Ritchie and jumped on him in an attempt to overpower the policeman and escape. A fierce fight ensued. It lasted approximately fifteen minutes before Ritchie eventually overcame the burglar and tied his feet with a clothes line. In the course of the struggle Ritchie was injured. A hard kick on his left temple produced a prominent swelling which Ritchie, the Force's oldest pensioner at ninety-one, still bears to this day. The second award was made to Constable Donald Dunnet in May 1910, for having, on several occasions, specially distinguished himself in rescuing persons from drowning.

To commemorate the Coronation of King George V and Queen Mary in 1911, there was a special issue of Police Medals for long and meritorious service. Ten were granted to the Aberdeen force and the recipients were Chief Constable William Anderson, Superintendent Charles Goodall, Inspectors Alexander McKay and George Wilson, Detective Alexander Clark, Sergeant William Garrow and Constables Charles Dunbar, Peter Henderson, James Low and George Murray.

January 1912, saw the introduction of battery-operated electric lamps. These replaced the hitherto indispensable oil lamps but many of the night-men were loath to part with their old oil lamps, which had served them so well and for so long. Of course, the new lamps were much more reliable. They did not require regular cleaning and re-fuelling!

The following year was one of increased activity by the Women's Suffrage Movement, 'The Suffragettes'. Many of its members were militant and sometimes caused disturbance, destruction and violence. Fortunately, Aberdeen was not affected much by their activities, but women's footprints at the seat of a fire, which badly damaged part of Ashley Road Public School during the early hours of Saturday, 3 May 1913, led the police to suspect it was the work of some militant members of the movement.

Prior to February 1914, an anomaly existed in the rank structure of the Force. 'Detective Officer' was not regarded as a rank, yet holders of the appointment were paid more than Sergeants. Anderson decided to follow the example of Edinburgh and Glasgow and to introduce to the C.I.D. the rank structure of the Uniform Department. He obtained authority to promote the six Detective Officers to the rank of Inspector. The total strength of the Force was then two hundred: Chief Constable, Deputy Chief Constable, three Superintendents, one Chief Inspector, twelve Inspectors, nineteen Sergeants and one hundred and sixty-three Constables.

Salaries and wages were revised and soon afterwards that of the Deputy Chief Constable was raised to three hundred and twenty pounds; and the maxima for Superintendents, Chief Inspectors and Inspectors were set at two hundred and eighty, one hundred and ninety and one hundred and fifty-five pounds, respectively. The top weekly rate for Sergeants was raised to two pounds four shillings and elevenpence while Constables were to be paid from one pound seven shillings and fivepence to one pound seventeen shillings and elevenpence, according to class and length of service.

In March 1914, the Chief Constable convinced his Committee that the Headquarters in Lodge Walk was much too small for the Force. The City Architect was instructed to prepare plans to extend the building at the north end towards Queen Street. This was done and an

Phaeton 1891

Prison Van 1891

Police Ambulance 1938

Patrol Car 1939

Team System Fleet 1949

Panda Vans 1968

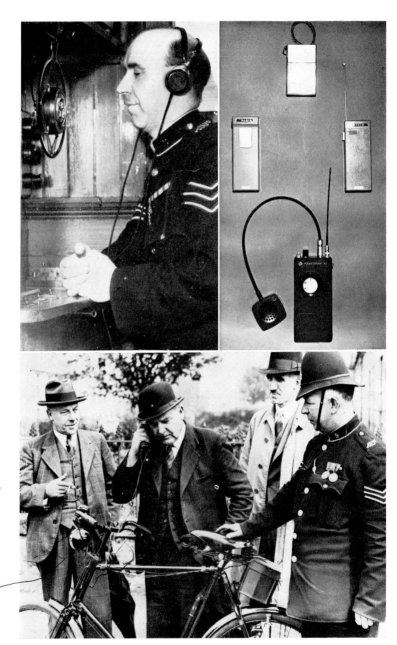

Wireless Transmitter   Personal Radios
1935   1965–71

Radio Bicycles 1937

extension costing a little over two and a half thousand pounds was approved. It provided on the ground floor, a clothing store, dining room, kitchen, precognition rooms and toilet facilities; while the first floor included a museum, property store and photographic department. In November of the same year, a further property acquisition was agreed, when the Mile-End Fire Station was purchased and converted for use as a Police sub-station.

The coming of motor transport led to a further alteration at the headquarters buildings, when the prison-type gateway to the courtyard at the rear was removed to provide easy access for the Force's first motorised ambulance, a 15 horse-power Wolseley costing in the region of four hundred and fifty pounds. In July, a contract had been entered into with the firm of Claude Hamilton (Aberdeen) Ltd, to supply the Force with its first motorised prison van — a 20.3 horse-power Wolseley — but the outbreak of the First World War in 1914 postponed its delivery for the duration.

During the war, seventy-eight members of the Force joined the Armed Forces. Twelve were killed or died of wounds and nine were discharged on medical grounds. The names of those who served are given in the Roll of Honour (Appendix VII.)

Notwithstanding the depleted state of the Force, the city was satisfactorily policed during the war years. For this, credit was due in no small measure to the three hundred and fifty citizens who became Special Constables and to the long hours worked by regular members of the Force. Daily tours of duty lasted ten hours, only occasional days off were granted, leave was severely curtailed, and men due to retire on pension were retained in the service.

A distressing accident resulting in the death on duty of forty-year-old Constable George Craib, 121 Huntly Street, occurred in August 1915. Craib had attended an accident in Holburn Street and had taken an injured girl to the Royal Infirmary for treatment in the ambulance. On leaving the building Craib was seen to fall heavily. His head struck a concrete pavement knocking him unconscious. He died later in hospital. The Police Surgeon certified that Craib had died from the effects of an injury 'received in the course of his duty, without his own default'.

The Police were also called upon to report on another tragic death in June 1916, the outcome of a foolhardy escapade. The victim was a thirty-three-year-old ship's cook, Foster Nelson Sharman of 146 South Esplanade East. To settle an argument as to who was the better swimmer, Sharman and a friend had climbed on to the parapet of Wellington Suspension Bridge and jumped into the River Dee. His friend reached the bank safely but Sharman got into difficulties and George Ogilvie, boat hirer, went to his assistance. He towed Sharman to the bank and applied artificial respiration. Both swimmers were taken to the Royal Infirmary for treatment, but Sharman was found to be dead on arrival.

Feelings ran high in Aberdeen during the course of the 1917 General Election campaign. On 19 March, the Labour leader, Ramsay Macdonald, was shouted down at a meeting in the Music Hall and two days later the 'Peace by Negotiation' candidate for the South Aberdeen Constituency, Mr Pethwick Lawrence, encountered considerable hostility at a Music Hall meeting. A large and angry crowd gathered in South Silver Street where a section armed themselves with pieces of iron railing which they hurled at the side entrance to the hall. Others pelted officials with rotten eggs and fruit and several windows were broken. Police reinforcements were called. Batons were drawn, the crowd driven back and the street cleared. It would seem that the pacifist views of Ramsay Macdonald and Pethwick Lawrence did not endear them to a population, many of whom had lost relatives in the war.

The Police (Weekly Rest Day) (Scotland) Act, 1914, came into force on 1 August 1918. As the title implies, it required Police Authorities to grant policemen one day off weekly, except on occasions of emergency. Previous to the outbreak of war, policemen had been granted weekly leave at the rate of one Sunday in three and one week day every three weeks.

The sharp rise in the cost of living during the war placed the police of the country in a precarious financial position. A standard rate of pay had not yet been introduced and Scots policemen fared even worse than their English and Welsh counterparts. The situation was improved in April 1919, when revised scales of pay were introduced giving Constables a commencing wage of two pounds, three shillings weekly.

The rank and file, however, were far from satisfied. 'The Police and Prison Officers' Union' had been formed, and in 1918 a number of Metropolitan policemen withdrew their labour because Union recognition had been denied by the Government. The strike — an irregular action on the part of a disciplined body — resulted in the setting up of a Commission of Inquiry under the chairmanship of Lord Desborough to review police pay and conditions of service. Its findings contained in 'The Desborough Report' led to the implementation of conditions which, for the first time, made the Service attractive to young men of education and ambition.

The Police Act, 1919, followed. It debarred police officers from joining a union, but provided for the setting up of the Police Federation, a representative body with branches in every Force. Membership of 'The Police and Prison Officers' Union' thus became illegal and policemen who had joined were required either to resign or be dismissed. The 'Union' called its members out on strike, but only in London and Liverpool did substantial numbers withdraw their services. A general warning had been issued that officers refusing to work would be instantly dismissed and accordingly all the strikers were discharged when they failed to report for duty. In Liverpool, criminals indulged in widespread looting, a development which illustrated to many the necessity of having an efficient and contented Police Force.

The 'Desborough' conditions took effect on 1 April 1919. Constables throughout the country were paid at the standard weekly rate of three pounds ten shillings on appointment rising to four pounds fifteen shillings after twenty-two years' service. Higher ranks got similar increases. The Chief Constable's maximum salary was raised to nine hundred and an Inspector's to three hundred and fifty pounds.

The report also recommended that all ranks should be provided with rent free housing; that a weekly boot allowance of one shilling and sixpence be paid; that an eight-hour working day be introduced; and that all ranks be entitled to retire after twenty-five or thirty years' service, with pensions at the rate of one half, and two thirds pay, respectively.

A deputation from the Aberdeen Town Council attended conferences of Police Authorities held in Edinburgh to consider the report, with instructions to oppose the provision of rent free housing. The Council maintained their opposition until July 1920, when they received a circular from the Secretary of State pointing out that 'with respect to the provision of free housing or a system of rent allowances in connection with the Police, adequate provision in this matter will be regarded in future as a condition precedent to the payment of the Government grant'.

In December 1919, the Council deliberated on a resolution from the local branch of the National Council of Women of Great Britain and Ireland on the recruitment of women police but the Council decided there was no necessity to employ women police in Aberdeen. One of the main factors taken into account was that since 1914 the Police Department had employed a 'Court Sister' who was undertaking duties in relation to women and children for which policewomen would be desirable.

In June 1920, members of the Force were granted permission to place in the Muster Room at Headquarters a granite tablet in memory of their colleagues who had fallen in the War. It bore the names

Sergeant George Duncan, Gordon Highlanders
Corporal Thomas Ogg, M.M., Gordon Highlanders
Lance Corporal Alexander Bremner, Gordon Highlanders
Private Gordon Douglas, Gordon Highlanders
Sapper Alexander Wood, Royal Engineers
Corporal Arthur Mortimer, Seaforth Highlanders
Private Robert Coutts, London Regiment
Gunner James Cruickshank, R.F.A.
Gunner James McIntosh, R.F.A.
Gunner James Pirie, R.F.A.
Gunner George Gerrard, R.F.A.
Signaller David Grieve, R.G.A.

One of the provisions of the Police Pensions Act, 1921, which came into operation in August of that year, was to cause the retiral on pension of Constables and Sergeants at the age of fifty-five; Inspectors and Superintendents at sixty and Chief Constables and Assistants at sixty-five. The immediate effect on the Force was the retirement of an Inspector, a Sergeant and seven Constables.

The valuable service rendered to the community by the Special Constabulary during the First World War was recognised by the Town Council in the award of certificates testifying to their loyalty and patriotism. In September 1921, H.M. Government went a step further by issuing two hundred and seventy-six Special Constabulary Long Service Medals for presentation to eligible members of the Force.

The reluctance of the Town Council to pay a non-pensionable cost of living bonus led to one of the most embarrassing situations in the history of the Force. Actually, the dispute began in December 1920, when policemen in England and Wales were awarded such a bonus. The Scottish Secretary recommended a similar payment to Scots policemen but several Councils, including Aberdeen, objected and protested against undue interference from the Government. In October 1921, despite an appeal from the Scottish Secretary, Aberdeen and a number of other Police Authorities still refused to pay the bonus or even to compromise. Thus in February 1922, an appeal from the Aberdeen Branch Board of the Scottish Police Federation was rejected by the Watching Committee, who even refused to meet a deputation on the subject. In March, the Scottish Secretary again urged payment, pointing out that the majority of Police Authorities had now done so. His letter concluded 'In the event of any Police Authority finally deciding not to pay a bonus the question will arise of making a deduction from the grant payable to them in respect of police expenditure generally'. The official whip had cracked but the Town Council resolved that it would pay the bonus only if compelled to do so.

The bonus remained unpaid and on the occasion of the Annual Inspection of the Force by His Majesty's Inspector, Lieutenant-Colonel Ferguson, in the Duthie Park, on Wednesday, 17 May 1922, the men on parade out-maneouvred the Town Council by taking the unprecedented step of presenting the following petition:

'The Inspectors, Sergeants and Constables of this Force contend that they are being unfairly and unjustly treated in regard to the bonus, when it is considered that out of a total of 66,000 policemen in this country, about 65,000 have already been paid and 200 of the 1000 still unpaid are members of this Force. This is not in accordance with the scheme of standardisation recommended by the Desborough Committee or the findings of the Scottish Police Council.

They consider that the payment of this bonus is but the honouring of a just and legal point and feel that the contentment conducive to efficiency will not exist in this Force and that its members will have a just cause for complaint unless the grievance is remedied.'

Lieutenant-Colonel Ferguson accepted the petition and promised to bring the matter to the attention of the Secretary of State.

In April 1923, serious trouble broke out amongst Aberdeen fishermen who had gone on strike in protest against the landing of German-caught fish at the Port.

On Sunday evening, 1 April, the police were called to the Fish Market where strikers had stopped porters entering the market to unload a German vessel. Tempers flared and an Inspector and one of the porters were assaulted. Reinforcements were called and a large body of police, with batons drawn, charged the strikers and cleared them from the vicinity of the Market. About eleven o'clock, two porters, who had tried to enter the Market by a side door, were set upon by the strikers. One escaped but the other was assaulted before the police could intervene. However, this was only a prelude to uglier incidents the next day. On Monday morning, about three thousand strikers assembled at Point Law. They marched to the Fish Market and took possession of it. They removed the hawsers from three German trawlers, casting them adrift and bombarding the crews with fish and pieces of ice. A fourth German vessel, in the process of unloading was also cast adrift, the fish which had been landed being dumped in the dock.

About eighty policemen were sent in. They formed a semi-circle in front of the German boats and as the strikers advanced, the order to draw batons was given. As contact was made, the Constables moved forward together. Batons were used to drive the strikers back and several fell and were trampled upon by their fellow strikers. When they had gained about two hundred yards, the police contingent reformed and charged again. This time, the strikers rapidly dispersed and so little damage was done. A few policemen were injured, fortunately none of them seriously.

Disorder of a vastly different kind required police attention in July and August 1925, this time in the Council Chamber! The central character was that colourful figure, Councillor Fraser Macintosh, whose behaviour led to his eviction from the Chamber on more than one occasion. The scene on Tuesday, 18 August, was perhaps the most memorable. Following exchanges with the Lord Provost, Sir Andrew Lewis, Councillor Macintosh was ordered to leave the Chamber. He refused and the police were called. An Inspector and four Constables arrived and the Councillor was led out with his thumbs in the armpits of his waistcoat, while another Councillor sang 'For he's a jolly good fellow!' Five minutes later, Macintosh made a surprise return to the Chamber by the door leading from the Town and County Hall. The Lord Provost was not amused. He recalled the policemen and advised the Chief Constable to see they carried out their duties, putting 'that man' out of the house and keeping him out. Councillor Macintosh was led away quietly.

Later, when the excitement had died down, there was a loud crash at the door. 'Fraser Mac's' head and shoulders appeared in the opening! He had been seized by the two Constables, his collar had been torn, his red tie dishevelled and the back of his neck bruised.

Councillor Macintosh had been evicted under similar circumstances on 6 July 1925. Following this he had raised an action against the Lord Provost, Magistrates and Town Council of the City of Aberdeen and William Anderson, Chief Constable, for the sum of twenty pounds as 'moderate reparation and solatium for the suffering and indignity to which the complainer was subjected by the illegal action of the defenders or their servants'. The action was called in the small debt court on 10 September 1925. A legal argument arose as to whether it was competent and relevant to deal with the matter there. However, during the argument, Councillor Macintosh suddenly withdrew the case and in reply, Sheriff Dallas remarked, 'I congratulate you'. A remarkable character, Fraser Macintosh's portrait now adds a note of colour to one of the Committee Rooms in the Town House.

During 1926, the Chief Constable focused his attention on ways of making the best use of his manpower, many of whom were becoming increasingly involved in traffic control. He proposed to introduce a comprehensive Police Box System and studied this in operation in Newcastle, Sunderland, Manchester and Glasgow. Already eleven police boxes had been built and in 1929, authority was granted to erect a further twenty-seven, thus providing the city with thirty-eight, all of them erected on carefully selected sites. (Appendix VIII.) Each box was equipped with a telephone linked to Headquarters. This could be used by policemen inside the box and by the public from the outside, the public simply having to open a small door and follow the printed instructions. The telephones were primarily intended for use as an alarm for Police, Ambulance or Fire Brigade. Selected boxes were termed 'Beat Boxes' to be used by 'Beat Constables' as their Headquarters and for reporting on and off duty.

In July 1927, Major William David Allan, O.B.E., who earlier that year had become His Majesty's Inspector of Constabulary, paid his first visit to the Force and showed a keen interest in the proposed re-organisation. Born at Elgin, Morayshire, in 1879, Major Allan had been educated at Elgin Academy and had had a distinguished army career. He had been commissioned in the Black Watch Regiment and seen active service in the South African War and the First World War. He became Chief Constable of Bootle, Lancashire in 1919 and a year later took command of the Argyllshire Constabulary, the post he held when he succeeded Lieutenant-Colonel Ferguson.

In August 1927, following the sudden death of the Court Sister, Mrs Agnes Peat, Anderson suggested the appointment of the city's first policewoman, and approval to do so was given in January 1928. She was twenty-seven-year-old Miss Margaret Flaws, a domestic servant from New Spynie, Elgin, who took up the appointment on 6 July 1928. She had been required to undergo and pass the same medical and educational examinations as male candidates and was paid three pounds weekly on appointment, rising to four pounds five shillings after twenty-two years service, plus an allowance of five shillings weekly in lieu of uniform.

Miss Flaws proved a great asset to the Force. Her kind and understanding manner was reflected in the many cases involving women

and children with which she was primarily concerned, while her untiring efforts to assist underprivileged families will long be remembered.
She was promoted Sergeant in 1952.

By September 1928, the problem of traffic control was occupying
much of the Chief Constable's attention. He visited Edinburgh and
Leeds to study the effectiveness of the new 'day coloured light signals'
and his recommendation and that of his committee led to the installation in May 1929 of the city's first traffic lights at the junction of George
Street and Hutcheon Street.

On 20 January 1930, following a recommendation by the Chief
Constable, the Town Council resolved to adopt selected sections of
the Burgh Police (Scotland) Act, 1892, the most important being
Section 80, which provided that:

'The Chief Constable and Constables shall have all the powers and
privileges which any Constable or police officer duly appointed has
by virtue of the common law or by statute in any county in which
such burgh is wholly or partly situated, and in any burgh con-
tiguous or adjacent to such burgh and in any harbour, bay, loch
or anchorage, within or adjoining such burgh or county.'

Prior to this, Aberdeen policemen had no jurisdiction beyond the city
boundary, a ludicrous position when the use of motor vehicles was on
the increase.

In 1930, His Majesty's Inspector of Constabulary, the now Lieutenant
Colonel Allan was transferred to a similar position in England
and Wales and Brigadier-General R. M. Dudgeon, D.S.O., M.C.
succeeded him in Scotland. Robert Maxwell Dudgeon of Gargen,
Dumfries, had been a distinguished soldier. He had joined the Queen's
Own Cameron Highlanders as a 2nd Lieutenant in 1900, and had served
in the South African War earning the Queen's Medal with five clasps.
During the First World War, he had served in France and Germany
as a Brigadier. He was wounded, and Mentioned in Dispatches five
times. He was awarded the Military Cross and Legion of Honour in
1915 and the Distinguished Service Order in 1917. He retired in 1920
with the rank of Brigadier-General and in 1924, became Governor of
His Majesty's Prison, Edinburgh, the position he held when appointed
H.M. Inspector of Constabulary in Scotland. It was Dudgeon who, in
1932, suggested that all Scottish Police Forces should adopt a standard-
ised cap with the blue and white diced band which, until recent years,
was worn exclusively by Scottish Policemen.

In 1931, the office of Police Surgeon came under review. It will be
remembered that the first holder of the post was Dr Francis Ogston.

He had held office for fifty years, but as time went on, his successors found the police duties were making ever-increasing demands on their time, to such an extent that Dr Alexander Brown, who was appointed in 1929, was obliged to relinquish the post in March 1931. It appears Dr Brown reported the circumstances to the Aberdeen Branch of the British Medical Association because within two weeks of his resignation the local executive of that body made representations to the Council with regard to the duties and remuneration of the office.

The Watching Committee gave careful consideration to the representations made and also conferred with the Town Clerks of Dundee and Edinburgh. Thereafter, they resolved to make two appointments, a 'Casualty Surgeon' and a 'Police Surgeon', at salaries of fifty pounds and one hundred pounds respectively. Dr Robert Richards, Lecturer in Forensic Medicine at the University of Aberdeen, was appointed Casualty Surgeon and three months later Dr John Leiper was appointed Police Surgeon.

The Casualty Surgeon was required to attend, day or night, all cases where medical aid or examination was considered necessary by the Chief Constable, including the examination of victims of assault, insane persons being dealt with according to law and sudden and/or suspicious deaths. He was also required to testify in court whenever his professional evidence was required and to communicate daily with the Chief Constable.

The Police Surgeon was required to instruct Constables in First Aid to St Andrew's Ambulance Association certificate standard; to medically examine police recruits; to attend Town Council Meetings as required; and to attend Police Headquarters daily. He had also to examine Fire Brigade entrants and attend injured and sick firemen including the Firemaster and Deputy Firemaster.

On 3 August 1932, Chief Constable Anderson intimated his intention to retire.

'My Lord Provost, Ladies and Gentlemen,

I beg to give notice in terms of Section 2 of the Police Pensions Act, 1921, that it is my desire to retire from the office of Chief Constable of the City as of 23rd December, next — the 30th anniversary of the day on which I took charge of the Force. By that date, I shall have completed 42 years' police service and be 70 years of age.

I have the honour to be,
Your obedient servant,
(Signed) W. Anderson.'

In accepting his resignation, the Lord Provost said, 'Mr Anderson has held the high and responsible office of Chief Constable of the City for a period of thirty years. The office called for a combination of discipline and tact, for qualities of organisation and of ability to meet emergency, and Mr Anderson, by carrying out his duties efficiently and well, has earned the gratitude of the citizens of Aberdeen. I feel sure that the Council will join with me in wishing Mr Anderson many happy years of retirement to enjoy the leisure which he has so well earned.'

Chapter Twelve

1933-55

Anderson's deputy at the time of his retiral was Superintendent John McConnach, M.B.E., who had also served for forty-two years and was about to retire. Consequently the appointment of a new Chief Constable had to be given urgent consideration by the Town Council.

The post was widely advertised and twenty-two applications were received. A short leet of four was drawn up, including John McConnach's eldest son, James. The leet comprised:

James McConnach, Chief Constable, Newark-on-Trent.
William B. R. Morren, Superintendent, Edinburgh City Police.
Alexander C. Sim, Deputy Chief Constable, Aberdeenshire.
William R. Wilkie, Chief Constable, South Shields.

The Town Council selected James McConnach, but his appointment was subject to the approval of the Sheriff-Principal of the County and the Secretary of State. Approval was duly given and McConnach took up the appointment on 30 January 1933, at a salary of seven hundred and fifty pounds.

At the time of his appointment, McConnach was thirty-seven years of age and had been in the police service for seventeen years. He was a native of Aberdeen, having been educated at Broomhill Primary School and at Robert Gordon's College. On leaving school, he had worked in the office of the Procurator-Fiscal for Aberdeenshire until 1913, when he joined Grimsby Borough Police as a Constable. During the First World War, he served in the Scottish Horse and the Black Watch regiments, then in the Imperial Camel Corps in Egypt, as Staff-Sergeant and Courts Martial clerk.

After the war, McConnach returned to his post in Grimsby, being promoted Sergeant in 1920 and Inspector four years later.

In April 1927, he was appointed Chief Constable and Chief Officer of the Fire Brigade at Newark-on-Trent. There he completely re-organised the Police Force and devised a new method of policing the town. He introduced similar measures to the Fire Brigade and acquired for it the most up-to-date equipment.

News of the new Chief Constable's reforming zeal spread quickly and members of the Aberdeen Force awaited with some apprehension, the outcome of his initial review of the Force's affairs.

They had not long to wait. On 22 April 1933, McConnach submitted to the Town Council a report, 'Economies in Police Administration', which was received with misgivings by many members. The economies he recommended included reducing the number of senior ranks by a third, in effect by one Superintendent, two Lieutenants and three Inspectors, a saving of two thousand five hundred pounds annually. Against this, he proposed to recruit a second policewoman and four civilians at an annual cost of five hundred and fifty pounds. He desired also to spend a further nine hundred pounds equipping the Force with a further two motor cars, erecting a covered enclosure for vehicles, installing signal lamps on police boxes and providing photographic equipment for the Criminal Investigation Department. However, the net saving was still substantial and the Town Council and Secretary of State readily approved. The authorised strength of the Force was thereby reduced by five, to one hundred and ninety-five. It comprised one Chief Constable, one Superintendent and Deputy Chief Constable, two Lieutenants, eight Inspectors, twenty-three Sergeants and one hundred and sixty Constables.

In May 1933, the Secretary of State appointed a Departmental Committee with the following terms of reference: 'To consider the possibility of dividing Scotland into a small number of police administrative areas, or of consolidating contingency forces without increasing the cost to ratepayers.'

The Town Council maintained it was essential that Aberdeen City Police be retained as a separate force and that the amalgamation of the police forces of Aberdeenshire, Kincardineshire and Banffshire was one for the consideration of the County Councils concerned. Those counties and Moray and Nairn eventually formed in 1949 the Scottish North-Eastern Counties Constabulary, but the city force remains an independent unit.

Of course, the need to co-operate with other Forces in the pursuit of criminals and the recovery of stolen property was recognised. Consequently, in November 1933, the Town Council agreed to contribute eighty-one pounds annually towards the publication of the *Scottish Police Gazette*, which it was proposed to circulate, daily or at short intervals, to all police stations in the country.

By the end of his first year in office, McConnach realised that the drastic reduction in senior ranks which he had engineered on taking over, and the practice of senior officers not retiring when eligible for full pension, severely limited opportunities for promotion and in consequence lowered the morale of the men.

In an attempt to improve the situation, McConnach persuaded the Watching Committee to pass the following resolution:

'that members of the Force above the rank of Constable, on completing the period of service entitling them to retire on pension, shall be required to retire on the grounds that their retention in the Force would not be in the interest of efficiency.'

In a review of the Police Box System of policing introduced by his predecessor, McConnach noticed that several of the boxes were used only to house the telephone and first-aid kits. In view of this, in April 1934, he obtained approval to replace several of the boxes with Police micro-telephone pillars, which could be rented from the G.P.O. at two pounds per annum.

About this time a murder was committed in the city, which inflamed public feelings to a degree rarely experienced in this country.

The victim was eight-year-old Helen Priestly who lived with her parents in a tenement flat at 61 Urquhart Road. At lunchtime on Friday, 20 April 1934, her mother had sent her on an errand to a shop nearby. She had made the purchase but had disappeared on her way home.

Helen's body was found about five o'clock on Saturday morning, in a sack in the common lobby of the tenement where she lived. Her private parts had been interfered with in a manner suggesting criminal assault, but subsequent medical examination proved she had not been despoiled.

Suspicion fell on Alexander Donald and his wife Jeannie, neighbours in the same tenement. Of the eight families in the building, only the Donalds failed to take any interest in the tragedy, or take part in the search organised on the Friday night. Stranger still, after the finding of the body, they professed ignorance of the fact to a press reporter despite the fact they had been told of the grim discovery by a policeman.

Donald and his wife were arrested, but the husband was released later, when it had been established he had been at work at the time when Helen had died, between 1.30 and 2 p.m. on Friday.

Jeannie Ewen or Donald denied having committed the crime. To prove the case against her, scientific evidence was used on a scale hitherto unknown in Scotland. Sir Sydney Smith, Professor of Forensic Medicine at Edinburgh University, was called in. It was established that the sack in which Helen's body had been found was similar to others found in the Donalds' flat and that cinders adhering to the sack and to Helen's clothing had been washed! Washed cinders were also found in a box under Mrs Donald's sink! Of all the tenants in the house, only Mrs Donald had been in the habit of washing cinders, a practice which makes them more durable as fuel. Fibres taken from the sack and from the Donalds' flat were microscopically examined and twenty-five matched sets were found. Similar fibres could not be found in the other flats. Examination of the sack also revealed strands of Mrs Donald's hair.

Traces of blood, Group 'O', the most common, were found in the Donalds' flat, on the linoleum under the sink, on washing cloths and on newspapers. Helen's blood was Group 'O' but it contained certain uncommon properties. These properties were also present in the blood found in the flat.

Jeannie Donald professed her innocence throughout, but her conviction was secured by painstakingly prepared and convincingly presented scientific evidence. It took the jury only eighteen minutes to return a verdict of 'Guilty', and a sentence of death by hanging was passed. This was later commuted to Life Imprisonment.

The case has been described as 'the finest example of scientific detection in Scottish police history up to that time'. A detailed account of the investigations and trial has been published — *The Trial of Jeannie Donald*, edited by John G. Wilson, in the 'Notable British Trials Series'.

The use of radio as a means of communication in the Force began in 1934, when receivers were installed in two patrol vehicles. Because the radio frequency used was in the region of two megacycles, mobile transmitters were not fitted. However, their efficiency was poor owing to technical difficulties. In fact, to be efficient, vehicle aerials would have had to be over one hundred feet long!

These early moves however, placed the Force in the forefront of police radio communications, and in November of that year, the Secretary of State authorised Aberdeen as one of the three police wireless stations in Scotland, the others being Edinburgh and Glasgow.

In December, application was made to the Minister of Transport for all streets in the city to be declared by Order 'built-up areas' so that the thirty miles per hour speed limit would apply. More traffic regulations followed: One-way Streets, Pedestrian Crossings and Unilateral Waiting parking restrictions.

In February 1935, the Bridge of Dee and Nigg, then in Kincardineshire, were incorporated into the city and to meet this additional commitment, the Force was increased by six to two hundred and one and the Kincardineshire Constabulary Police Stations at Bridge of Dee and Nigg were taken over.

Re-organisation of the Special Constabulary followed. A recruiting campaign was launched and the strength was raised to three hundred. They were equipped with a cap, staff, armlet and whistle. A new training programme, designed to make the 'Specials' a more efficient force, was introduced, part of which required 'Specials' to perform frequent spells of duty alongside regular policemen. The value of the training was not fully appreciated until a few years later, when during the Second World War, the limited resources of the regular force was stretched to breaking point.

To many policemen throughout the country, the name of Aberdeen City Police is linked with the publications *Scottish Criminal Law, Police Duties and Procedure* and *Road Traffic Law* which have been the instruction and reference manuals of the Scottish Police Forces since 1952.

The books, which are loose-leafed and amended twice yearly, originated in that form in 1936. In January, the Chief Constable was authorised to obtain three hundred copies of the proposed *Instruction Book* — the fore-runner of the *Scottish Criminal Law* — and on 20 August, it was issued to all members of the Force. It was of a more comprehensive character than any of the manuals of instruction hitherto produced, but it excluded legislation on road traffic matters which were made the subject of a separate volume, issued later that year.

The value of the *Instruction Book* soon became evident and many policemen throughout the country made requests for copies. As the book was compiled primarily to meet local needs, these requests could not be granted.

Its companion volume, *Road Traffic Law*, was suitable for wider distribution and with the approval of the Town Council, it was offered for sale. The demand was such that by June 1937, the production costs had been repaid.

With the passing years, certain deficiencies in the books — not least of which was the omission of case law — became apparent, and accordingly in 1943, it was decided to revise completely the *Instruction Book* and make it available to members of other Forces. Similarly, *Road Traffic Law* was revised and re-issued in August 1952. This new edition was referred to in highly complimentary terms by Lord Goddard, Lord Chief Justice, in October of that year, during the course of an appeal being heard in the Queen's Bench Division of the Court of Criminal Appeal.

In the Foreword to *Scottish Criminal Law, Police Duties and Procedure*, the late Honourable Lord Guthrie, a Senator of the College of Justice in Scotland, wrote:

'This handbook will be invaluable to policemen of all ranks, since it contains a careful statement of their duties, of the manner in which these should be performed, and of the pitfalls to be avoided, and also selections from many of the statutes which they may be required to consider in the course of their work. It was a happy idea of the Chief Constable of Aberdeen City Police to issue it for the instruction of the force, but it has not merely a local value. It will be a useful work of reference for all policemen, for lawyers, social workers, local government officials and for all interested in the administration of our society and of its criminal law.'

Much of the work involved in the compilation of the original manuals was done by a serving member of the Force, Alexander Paterson, M.A., B.L. who joined in 1932, and became Deputy Chief Constable before moving to Salford as Chief Constable in 1949. When he died in 1967, he was Chief Constable of Leeds City Police, one of the very few Scottish trained police officers to be appointed Chief Constable of a force in England and Wales. His death came in rather tragic circumstances when, as Vice-President of the Association of Chief Police Officers, he collapsed whilst addressing the World Police Organisation in Tokyo.

By 1937, great progress had been made with police radio communications, and McConnach, ably assisted by Edward Ingram, the Force's first radio technician, undertook much of the pioneer work and gave Aberdeen a lead over other forces in this field. In April, the Town Council approved further investment in radio equipment, after McConnach had reported that good wireless communications had led to a reduction in the number of housebreakings in the city.

The increased expenditure was to provide an improved mains transmitter, two portable transmitters and to equip ten police bicycles with receivers. McConnach explained, 'The fitting of these cycles with wireless would enable Headquarters to be in constant communication with the Sergeants and Constables on the outlying beats. As the city extends, so does the call for more supervision, and at the present time at least, the fitting up of these cycles will enable the policing of these districts to be done more efficiently, and postpone the date when application will have to be made for an increase in the Force'.

McConnach also reported that it was possible to obtain duplex or two-way communication between cars and Police Headquarters on the ultra-short wave-band, a factor he considered important in connection with Air-Raid Precautions, for if the existing telephone services were put out of action, it would provide a supplementary means of communication. However, duplex or two-way working was not possible on the 145 metre wave-band then in use and he requested that the Post Office be asked to allocate an ultra-short wave-length for the Force.

The Town Council and Secretary of State approved the proposals set out in McConnach's report, which incurred expenditure of one hundred and thirty-five pounds.

The receivers fitted to the pedal cycles were three valve miniatures and by this means, Sergeants and officers on patrol in outlying districts were advised of incidents requiring their attention. Several tales are told as to the effectiveness of this equipment. One Sergeant, when asked how the receiver was operating, said he heard of a fire in Liverpool and of a warehouse raid in London, but had no idea of what had been going on in Aberdeen!

On 15 November 1937, the Chief Constable's administration of the Force was called into question when the Town Council passed a motion — 'that there be instituted and conducted an enquiry into the Chief Constable's administration of the Police Force with special reference to the disturbance at the Market Stance on 3 October, 1937.' The matter did not rest there. The Aberdeen Branch of The National Unemployed Workers Movement wrote a strongly worded letter to the Secretary of State protesting against police action:

'Sir,

This mass meeting of Aberdeen Workers, held under the auspices of the above-named organisation, protest emphatically against the attitude adopted by the Police at a recent meeting held by the British Union of Fascists in the public market place on October, 3rd.

The Police, under the instruction of Deputy Chief Constable Groat, drew their batons and struck down many defenceless workers, who had been attentively listening to another meeting which was then in progress.

Such tactics on the part of the Police warrants an immediate inquiry being made by your Department, which we demand should be done. We furthermore demand the immediate dismissal of the Deputy Chief.

Yours,

(Sgd) George Esson, Acting Secretary.'

A similar letter was sent to the Scottish Secretary by Aberdeen Trades Council.

The terms of the resolution requesting an enquiry, passed by the Town Council, was sent to the Secretary of State, but he pointed out, 'If the Town Council consider that there is a *prima facie* case for holding an enquiry into the Chief Constable's administration of the Force, it is their duty, as the disciplinary authority in relation to the Chief Constable and as the body responsible to the citizens of Aberdeen for the control of the police, to institute and conduct the enquiry themselves'.

A sub-committee was appointed to consider the matter. The Town Clerk prepared for its guidance a memorandum on the relationship between the Town Council and the Police Force. Legal opinion was obtained from the Dean of Faculty, Mr W. S. Patrick, K.C. and finally, on 31 March 1938, the resolution of 15 November was rescinded.

By April 1938, war clouds were gathering, and police forces throughout the country were required to undertake the organisation and training of personnel in Air Raid Precautions work. An Inspector, a Sergeant and two Constables were released from ordinary duties for A.R.P. work, in particular the recruiting and training of two thousand, five hundred Air Raid Wardens. The Chief Constable was appointed A.R.P. Controller, a post which he was to hold until June 1942.

In February 1939, the Secretary of State advised the Town Council to recruit more policemen to enable the Force to carry out A.R.P. work and the other emergency tasks which would arise in the event of war. He recommended setting up a full-time body of ex-policemen, or other suitable persons, to be known as the 'First Police Reserve'. He also suggested that greater use be made of the Special Constabulary.

The 'First Police Reserve' was an important part of the Government National Service Scheme and the Chief Constable was authorised to enrol forty members, each man receiving an annual retaining fee of five pounds and payment of approximately ten shillings daily. It was decided also to provide the Special Constabulary with uniform.

This reserve strength alone was not going to be sufficient for the heavy demands which would be placed on the Force under emergency conditions and the establishment of the Force was reviewed. In April 1939, it was increased by sixteen, to two hundred and seventeen — one Chief Constable, one Superintendent, four Lieutenants, eleven Inspectors, twenty-seven Sergeants and one hundred and seventy-three Constables. The number of civilian employees was also raised from nineteen to twenty-eight.

In June 1939, it was decided to extend Police Headquarters in Lodge

Walk by erecting a new wing at the north end of the building. In connection with the Air Raid Precautions Scheme for the city, it had not been possible to find suitable accommodation for a main control and report centre and Police Headquartrs, in its existing form, was indequate. Indeed for some time past, it had been realised that it was unsuitable for a modern police force. The new three-storey wing provided, in protected premises on the ground floor, A.R.P. accommodation and telephone exchange; new offices for the Chief Constable on the top floor; improved departmental accommodation and emergency dormitories. The extension, which cost eight thousand, six hundred pounds, was completed in October 1940.

The Second World War suspended recruitment to the Force, delayed the retiral of men eligible for pension, led to the enlistment of a Police War Reserve Force, the formation of the Women's Auxiliary Police Corps and the Police Auxiliary Messenger Service, the employment of a number of Special Constables on full-time duty and the raising of the strength of the Special Constabulary to four hundred and fifty.

The war also raised the cost of living and in October 1940, the Government granted the police a supplementary allowance of five shillings weekly pointing out that it was in recognition of war conditions of service which were special to the police. Sergeants and Constables, who would normally have been eligible for overtime payment, or time-off in lieu, had to work up to twelve hours a day without recompense and also had to forfeit their right to a weekly rest day. A war duty allowance of three shillings a week to Constables and four shillings to Sergeants was also paid.

The emergency conditions focused attention on the police boxes at Fonthill Road, Mile-end, Torry and Leadside Road. These boxes being of timber construction did not provide adequate protection and in any case were too small for the purposes required of them. Consequently, in March 1941, approval was given to build in stone, new police sub-stations at Fonthill Road, Mile-end and Torry and for the lease and conversion of a shop at No. 23 Northfield Place as a sub-station.

A wartime event which required the deployment of a large force of police took place on 10 March 1941. This was the official opening of the new bridge over the River Dee at Allenvale and His Majesty King George VI, accompanied by Her Majesty the Queen, visited the city for the ceremony. They were met at the railway station by Lord Provost Thomas Mitchell, The Marquis of Aberdeen, Lord Lieutenant of the County and Mr Thomas Johnston, Secretary of State for Scotland. The party then made its way to the bridge where Her Majesty named the 'King George VI Bridge' and declared it open for public use. Thereafter, the Lord Provost suitably replied, paying tribute to: 'The steadfast courage displayed by Their Majesties and the sympathetic interest in the well-being of their people in these days of trial and suffering — an inspiration to all of us to stand fast until victory is won and peace once more established on the earth.'

After viewing the bridge, Their Majesties inspected representatives from the various Civil Defence Services, before proceeding to the Town House where His Majesty invested Dr Albert D. Imper, Commandant of the Special Constabulary, with the M.B.E.

During the war, the Police Force was a reserved occupation. Nevertheless, forty-eight members volunteered for service in the armed forces. The position of those policemen who wished to enlist deserves some comment. Officially, serving policemen were released only to serve as flying crew personnel in the Royal Air Force, and many, though not all, of the forty-eight referred to, offered their services as such. Six of the volunteers did not return and their names appear on the memorial tablet erected to their memory.

Gunner Alexander Barron, Royal Artillery
Flight-Lieutenant George Simpson Henderson, R.A.F.
Sergeant David Robertson Langlands, R.A.F.
Leading Aircraftsman Ronald McLeod, R.A.F.
Flying Officer William Reid, R.A.F.
Pilot Officer James Saunders, R.A.F.

On the 'Home Front', the Force, with limited resources, had to undertake many additional duties in the interests of national security and were prominent in rescue operations following enemy action. An unpopular task which they had to carry out was the enforcement of the Lighting (Restrictions) Order and the Defence Regulations. Hundreds of people were prosecuted yearly for failing to 'black-out' windows; for using unscreened torches in the streets; for failing to screen lights on vehicles; and for failing to immobilise motor vehicles.

If the citizens were shocked by many of the events and tragedies of the war, they were positively stunned when investigations at the Aberdeen Crematorium, Kaimhill, revealed circumstances, which, in due course, were described by Lord Norman in the Court of Criminal Appeal, in these words, 'I don't suppose that a case has come into these courts, which contains details so horrifying and so repugnant to ordinary decencies as this'.

Many Aberdonians, however, recalled a similar shameful case — 'The Nellfield Cemetary Scandals', of 1899 and for them 'The Coffin Lids Case' of 1944 added insult to injury.

Feelings in the North-East ran so high that, in the interests of justice, the trial, like that of Jeannie Donald in 1934, was held in Edinburgh. In both cases this unusual step was taken at the request of defence counsel who argued that the widespread indignation felt by the inhabitants of the North-East was such that a local jury could not reasonably be expected to be wholly impartial.

The central figures in the Crematorium scandal were the Managing Director, James Dewar, who was also a Town Councillor, and a local undertaker Alick George Forbes. During the course of the trial, it was alleged that coffin lids had been removed from coffins prior to cremations, and that on more than one occasion, unrelated bodies had been cremated together without the knowledge of relatives.

Some of the coffin lids and coffins had been used again, whilst in other cases, the wood had been used by Crematorium employees and others to make articles such as tea-trays, wireless cabinets, a bureau, boxes and even black-out shutters!

The removal of the lids was done quite openly. On one occasion a class of students witnessed a cremation and saw the lid being unscrewed and taken off. On that occasion, it was explained that the removal of the screws was to avoid damage to the interior of the furnace, while the removal of the lid was to facilitate cremation — explanations later refuted by other Crematoria Superintendents.

The accused stood trial before Lord Cooper, Lord Justice Clerk, at the High Court of Justiciary in Edinburgh, on 10 October 1944. The trial lasted four days. Dewar was found guilty of the theft of one thousand and forty-four coffin lids and two coffins, and sentenced to three years' Penal Servitude. Forbes was convicted of the reset of one hundred coffin lids and imprisoned for six months. Of course, widespread publicity was given to the case and the city's good reputation suffered badly, some Music Hall jesters being particularly cruel!

A year later the city again made the headlines in the local and national newspapers. The *Evening Express* of Wednesday, 12 December 1945 headlined, 'Grim find on Aberdeen Foreshore'; the next day's *Daily Mirror* carried 'Girl's Sawn-off Arm found on Shore'; while a *Daily Express* staff reporter compared the gruesome find with the famous Ruxton Murder case of 1935, which had been sparked off by the discovery in a Dumfries-shire ravine of the dismembered bodies of two women.

The case in question, 'The Betty Hadden Mystery', was never solved despite the most prolonged and intensive investigation in the history of the Force. It began on Wednesday, 12 December 1945, with the finding, on the foreshore on the south side of the Navigation Channel opposite Greyhope Road, of a forearm and hand later identified as that of seventeen-year-old Elizabeth Ann Craig or Hadden, who had lived with her widowed mother at 9 Manor Walk, Aberdeen.

Betty Hadden was a small brunette, who had been missing from her home for ten days. She was unemployed, but had worked at different times as an hotel kitchenmaid, a restaurant waitress, a factory-hand and as a fishworker.

She was last seen alive on Tuesday 11 December, and information obtained suggested that she may have been killed in the Torry District between midnight and 5 a.m. on Wednesday, 12 December. About two o'clock that morning, terror-stricken screams were heard from the area bounded by Mansefield Road, Victoria Road, St. Fittick's Road and the south bank of the River Dee. This area was systematically searched and residents closely questioned, but the murderer was never traced. Neither was the remainder of Betty's body, despite extensive searches and a thorough comb-out of the foreshore, docksides, wharves and banks of the River Dee. All shipping in the harbour, and vessels which had left recently, were checked and all along the four hundred miles of the east coast of Scotland, police officers co-operated in the search for human remains. A human leg was found near the Bullers of Buchan, on 23 December but it was a man's leg, probably that of a seaman. Over the years since the tragedy, fresh pieces of evidence have come to hand from time to time. All of this has been carefully checked and filed, but the results are inconclusive and the mystery remains.

On 30 November 1945, the Special Constabulary received the 'stand-down' from war duties, when all members over fifty-five years of age retired. At the same time an opportunity was given to all members to resign and quite a number took advantage of the concession. Whilst the authorised strength of the 'Specials' remained at three hundred and fifty, the actual strength, dropped to one hundred and twenty-four. Similarly, the Police War Reserve force decreased to thirty in number and the First Police Reserve to three. Forty-eight men were required to bring the regular force up to its pre-war strength of two hundred and thirty-four.

Throughout the country, the authorised strengths of police forces were increasing considerably, but not so in Aberdeen. McConnach decided to avoid an increase by making greater use of mechanical transport and introducing a new system of policing: 'The Aberdeen Team System of Policing' which came into being in April 1948, and will be mentioned later.

On 1 January 1946, Mr Sidney A. Kinnear succeeded Brigadier-General Dudgeon as His Majesty's Inspector of Constabulary for Scotland. Mr Kinnear, who had been His Majesty's Assistant Inspector of Constabulary for Scotland since 1942, was the first career police officer to become H.M. Inspector, he having joined Edinburgh City Police as a Constable in 1924.

In June of that year, the Scottish Chief Constables bestowed a singular honour on Mr McConnach. They elected him to take charge of the Scottish Police contingent at the Victory March in London, on 8 June. Only three Chief Constables in Great Britain took part in the parade, the other two representing England and Wales.

By 1946, the recruiting and training of new entrants had been given top priority. The Police Training Schools in Glasgow, Edinburgh and Aberdeen were recognised as the official training schools for Scotland. The Aberdeen school, staffed by members of the Force, was responsible for the training of recruits from the police forces of Aberdeenshire, Banffshire, Moray and Nairn, Kincardineshire, Inverness County and Burgh, Sutherlandshire, Caithness, Orkney and Shetland. This arrangement obtained until 9 September 1947, when it was agreed that the recruits from the North-East would be sent to the Scottish Police Training School at Whitburn, West Lothian, which had opened in the spring of that year. Training of policewomen was also carried on at Whitburn and the city's first three uniformed policewomen, recruited in 1947, received their initial training there.

The increased number of vehicles introduced by McConnach rendered inadequate the garaging and maintenance facilities at Lodge Walk, and in August 1947, the garage attached to the Civil Defence Depot in Claremont Place was acquired.

Developments had also taken place in the field of police radio communications. Since 1943, all police cars in the city had been fitted with high frequency radio equipment providing a rapid and efficient means of communication with Headquarters and sub-stations. The Force's network was recognised as one of the finest in the country and its facilities were also made available to the National Fire Service.

The years 1948 and 1949 were two of the most eventful in the history of the Force for it was then that the 'Team System of Policing' was introduced on an experimental basis in the northern part of the city on 4 April 1948, and then throughout the city on 1 January 1949.

The system was evolved in order to police the city more effectively and economically and take account of the shortage of manpower consequent on the Second World War, the rapid growth of new housing estates on the outskirts of the city, and a desire to improve the working conditions of members of the Force.

It was based on a series of principles: to deploy personnel to the best advantage; to encourage men's initiative, broaden their experience and remove the monotony of police work; and to improve the Force's effectiveness by the avoidance of routine and fixed methods, making the element of surprise paramount.

The city was divided into four districts: North, South, East and West. Each district was policed by a 'District Car' fitted with duplex V.H.F. radio. Radio contact was maintained with Headquarters where a Control Room was established to co-ordinate the police action required in relation to any incident.

One Sergeant and approximately twelve Constables, including the car crew were deployed on each district. Normally, the car crew consisted of the Sergeant, the driver and one or two Constables. It was the direct responsibility of the Sergeant to deploy the remainder of his 'District Constables' to the best advantage. To achieve this objective, the Sergeant, before each tour of duty, conferred with his Duty Inspector to ascertain in which areas men were to be deployed, this being determined largely by such factors as the incidence of crime, traffic accidents, traffic density, special events and occasions. In addition, an hour-to-hour appraisal was made by the supervisory officers to maintain good deployment.

To enable a Sergeant to make ready contact with Constables under his control, each district was divided up into a number of 'Areas of Responsibility'. Constables on areas were required by the Sergeant to be within view of the signal lamps at sub-stations, kiosks or pillars at twenty, thirty, forty or fifty-minute intervals. The radio system was operated through the telephone switchboard at Headquarters thus providing a direct two-way link between any telephone extension and the cars. Consequently, the Sergeant could contact a Constable at a sub-station by requesting the telephone operator to 'flash' the appropriate sub-station or kiosk at the pre-arranged time.

All radio calls passed were heard through a monitor in the Control Room, from where messages could also be passed to cars by 'radio-telephone'. Personnel in the Control Room were thus enabled to direct and control the action to be taken by any car going to, or arriving at, any incident.

Members of the public soon appreciated the speedy and efficient police service being provided and co-operated by making greater use of the '999' emergency service.

It was also acclaimed in police circles. The Committee on Police Conditions of Service, presided over by Lord Oaksey, drew attention to the 'Team System' stating that it appeared to have improved the working conditions and the morale of the men without sacrificing efficiency. It invited Chief Constables of all other forces to study the system. Enquiries were received from all over the world and officers from many police forces at home and abroad came to the city to see it in action. Several other forces adopted it, including Adelaide, Australia, whilst others adapted it to suit different conditions and requirements.

The introduction of the 'Team System' led to a revision in the strength of the Force. The number of policemen was reduced and the number of civilians increased. At the end of 1948, the establishment provided for one Chief Constable, one Chief Superintendent, one Superintendent, three Chief Inspectors, thirteen Inspectors, thirty-one Sergeants, one hundred and seventy Constables, eight Policewomen and fifty-one civilian auxiliaries. The fleet of vehicles required to meet the needs of the system was completed by the end of 1949. It consisted of fifteen saloon motor cars, three vans and a motor cycle.

On 5 July 1948, the National Health Service became operative and members of the Force were free to choose his or her own doctor. Accordingly the duties of the Police Medical Officer were restricted to the examination of recruits and those officers with prolonged illnesses or incapacitated through ill-health. No change was made in the duties of the Police Casualty Surgeon, who was required to attend where and when medical examination of any person or article was necessary for police purposes and to report thereon.

The Oaksey Committee on police conditions reported its findings in 1949. Unlike the Desborough Report of 1919, it had little impact on the service, although some of its recommendations were eventually embodied in Police Regulations. It concluded that the police were underpaid and suggested a new scale of pay which the Secretary of State approved. The new scale fell far short of expectations. The gross weekly pay of Constables ranged from five pounds five shillings to seven pounds, whilst the maxima for Sergeants and Inspectors was raised to eight pounds five shillings and nine pounds seventeen shillings and six pence, respectively, with corresponding increases for higher ranks.

During the first quarter of 1950, an adult patrol scheme was inaugurated in the city to ensure the safety of school children at street crossings. It was the first scheme of its kind to be sponsored by the Scottish Education Department. At the outset, twenty-five patrols were recruited — mostly pensioners or housewives. The value of the scheme was quickly recognised and more appointments followed.

In 1950 the first police housing programme was commenced. Approval was given for the erection of eighty-six houses, including four of special design for officers of and above the rank of Inspector. The provision of housing proved to be a great boon. Immediately it was known that they were to be built, there was a sudden stop to the drift away from the service of married men who had been disheartened by having to live apart from their families or in sub-let accommodation which, in many cases, was expensive and inadequate.

One of the major policing events of 1953 was the duties performed in connection with the celebrations marking the Coronation of Queen Elizabeth II, on 2 June. The procession route — Albyn Place to St. Machar Drive via Alford Place, Union Street, Castle Street and King Street — was a long one and stretched the manpower of the Force to capacity. Nevertheless, with the aid of the Special Constabulary, the crowds were marshalled in good order and the co-operation of members of the public helped in no small measure to make the occasion a memorable one. The other events held during Coronation Week also required police attention, the River Dee pageant in particular attracting large crowds.

In the 1954 New Year's Honours list Chief Constable McConnach was awarded a C.B.E. in recognition of his outstanding public service. He also held the King's Police Medal, awarded on 3 July 1944, and a number of foreign awards.

Almost exactly a year later, on 23 January 1955, members of the Force and the public alike were shocked by the news of Mr McConnach's death, after a short illness, at the age of fifty-eight. In a fitting tribute to his memory the *Evening Express* of 24 January, described Mr McConnach as a 'Police Chief who pioneered policing methods which brought national and international recognition to the City'.

Chapter Thirteen

1955-63

On the death of Mr McConnach — in accordance with the provisions of the Aberdeen Corporation (Administration, Finance, etc.) Order, 1939 — Alexander John Matheson, M.B.E., the Deputy Chief Constable became 'Chief Officer of Police'. He continued in this capacity until 4 July 1955, when he was appointed Chief Constable, at a salary of one thousand six hundred and fifty pounds.

Other applicants who had been considered for the post were Superintendent William Hunter, Edinburgh City Police; Chief Constable Andrew Meldrum, Angus; and Chief Superintendent Robert Pithie, Scottish North-Eastern Counties, Deputy Commandant, Scottish Police College.

A native of Inverness, Mr Matheson had joined the Aberdeen Force as a Constable on 25 May 1926, and was the last locally trained officer to rise through the ranks and become Chief Constable. In the future, regulations were to require that a police officer could not be appointed Chief Constable in his own force without having had at least two years' experience as a senior officer elsewhere.

The new Chief Constable's first year in office was highlighted by royal visits and with three cases of homicide. In August, en route to Balmoral Castle, Her Majesty the Queen disembarked from the Royal Yacht *Brittania* at Matthews Quay and visited Broadford Works, The Royal Aberdeen Hospital for Sick Children and the South Church of St Nicholas. The following week, His Royal Highness the Duke of Gloucester opened Headquarters for the Order of St John in Albyn Place and later presented new Colours to the 4/7th Battalion, The Gordon Highlanders, T.A.

Of the three cases of homicide referred to, the first occurred on 19 February, when an Aberdeen man, on his 23rd birthday, was apprehended for murdering his wife by throttling her in a house in Ferrier Crescent. The man, William Henry McKerron, appeared before the High Court in May. Pleading guilty to a reduced charge of culpable homicide, he was sentenced to twelve years' imprisonment. Next, on

14 October, the police were called to a house in the former Castlehill Barracks, where a young woman had died while undergoing an illegal operation. Consequently, at the High Court in November, a woman was sentenced to three years' imprisonment on a charge of culpable homicide. The third case arose from an association in Glasgow between a young married man and an eighteen-year-old girl. Both came to Aberdeen where the girl gave birth to a child in the Maternity Hospital. However, on 8 September in their lodgings in Powis Crescent, the man, Glaswegian, Robert James Boyle, smothered the child, later throwing it into the Harbour. He was arrested for the murder in Glasgow, appeared before the High Court in February 1956, was found guilty and sentenced to death. The sentence was later commuted to one of Life Imprisonment.

Reduced working hours for policemen in the form of one rest day in every fortnight, in addition to the weekly rest day, became operative on 5 September 1955. Manpower difficulties were thus created and approval was given for an immediate increase of one Inspector, three Sergeants and fifteen Constables, making the authorised strength of the force two hundred and forty-seven: one Chief Constable, one Chief Superintendent, one Superintendent, three Chief Inspectors, fourteen Inspectors, thirty-five Sergeants and one hundred and ninety-two Constables.

On 7 January 1957, Dr Robert Richards resigned as Police Casualty Surgeon on account of ill-health. He had held the post since 1931. The Town Council recorded their appreciation of his long and distinguished service and appointed Dr William Thomson Hendry to the post. He had been Dr Richard's deputy since 1955.

About this time, further experiments were being conducted in the field of police radio communications. As more and more people acquired television sets and V.H.F. radio receivers, police radio messages were being intercepted and evidence came to hand that un-authorised use was being made of the content of some messages. In one instance, it was found that an outbreak of fire in an office had probably been caused by an overheated radio receiver which had been tuned to the frequency of the police radio network.

To counter this interception, equipment for scrambling messages was fitted to several police vehicles, but the refined nature of the equipment and its high cost led to the abandonment of this experiment. Instead, police messages were curtailed in text so that they could be passed quickly and understood only by policemen.

Matheson was convinced that the efficiency of the Force was being adversely affected by the lack of manpower and he sought authority to recruit a further forty-nine men. The Town Council and Secretary of State authorised a further twenty Constables and five Cadets, making the strength, at December 1957, two hundred and seventy officers and men, and fifty-six civilian auxiliaries.

The Cadets were recruited during the summer of 1957. One hundred and seventy-six boys applied and the five successful applicants came from senior secondary schools. They underwent a three-weeks training course during which emphasis was placed on their physical fitness. They were then posted to the departments in the Force, being mainly employed in clerical duties and as telephone operators.

1958 was another year for homicides, three cases being reported. On 1 May, a man was arrested on a charge of murdering a trawl fisherman in the dock area. The charge was subsequently reduced to one of culpable homicide, but eventually, on instructions from the Crown Office, proceedings were dropped. The next case occurred during the evening of 21 July, when twenty-six-year-old labourer Eric Pirie Smith Stephen murdered his wife in their home in Ferrier Crescent, the woman being found dead in bed with a cloth ligature round her neck. Stephen was found guilty of murder and sentenced to Life Imprisonment. On 18 August, a mother of ten children was shot by her husband in her home at Rosehill Farmhouse and died later in hospital. Her husband, fifty-year-old lorry driver William McLeman Whyte, who had been living apart from the family, was arrested and charged with murder. He was found to be insane in bar of trial at a subsequent sitting of the High Court.

On 1 October 1957, Her Majesty's Inspector of Constabulary, Mr Sidney A. Kinnear was appointed Commandant of the Scottish Police College, Tulliallan Castle, Kincardine-on-Forth, Clackmannanshire. He was replaced as H.M. Inspector by the ex-Chief Constable of Lanarkshire, Mr Thomas Renfrew c.b.e., b.l.; his first official visit to the Aberdeen Force taking place on 6 March 1958.

In March 1958, the Minister of Transport and Civil Aviation published a report underlining the importance of Cycling Proficiency Training for school children. In collaboration with the Director of Education, a pilot scheme of this nature was introduced soon afterwards at Kaimhill School. Initially fifteen pupils were trained by members of the Traffic Department and all gained proficiency certificates and badges. The value of this form of training in preventing accidents was soon recognised and, with the aid of school-teacher instructors, the scheme expanded and by 1962 had embraced all the schools in the city. In order to stimulate interest in safe cycling, a local businessman gifted a cup 'The Nixon Trophy' to be awarded annually in June to 'The Aberdeen Young Cyclist of the Year'.

Towards the end of 1959 an experiment in training child cyclists at the Aberdeen School for the Deaf was conducted by a member of the Traffic Department. The pioneers were four deaf children who successfully passed the test. The work necessitated translating the Highway Code, so that it could be understood by deaf children, an experiment which attracted the attention of the Royal Society for the Prevention of Accidents and led to the publication in 1961, by the National Institute for the Deaf, of a 'Highway Code for Deaf Children'. It was compiled by the city policeman who had originated the idea.

It is worthy of recall at this juncture that the value of road safety training for school children had been recognised in Aberdeen in 1933, when Chief Constable McConnach introduced to most Aberdeen schools a scheme entitled 'Road Safety for School Children'.

The Force's last link with another form of transport, horse riding, was broken in January 1959, when the Chief Constable was authorised to dispose of 'a considerable number of items of saddlery, which had not been used for at least twenty years'. The introduction of mechanical transport had removed the need for a mounted section, although many of the larger police forces still maintain such a body for crowd control and ceremonial occasions. It was an embarassing incident at a ceremonial occasion on Saturday, 4 September 1937, which had led to the disbandment of the Mounted Section. The occasion was the official opening of St Katherine's Club, West North Street, by H.R.H. The Duchess of Gloucester. As was the practice, the horses were on hire from a local riding stables and consequently were not highly trained in crowd control duties. At the event, Constable Tam Grubb, on 'June' suffered acute embarrassment when his mount shied and backed into the Royal car, leaving a sizeable dent in one of the wings with her hindquarters!

In May 1959, Her Majesty Queen Elizabeth, The Queen Mother, visited the city and carried out several engagements: the opening of the Beach Boulevard; the receiving of the Freedom of the City; and the opening of the widened Bridge of Don. The following month, The Queen Mother again visited the city for the Royal Highland Show at Hazlehead and the opening of a new extension to the Royal Aberdeen Asylum for the Blind. The police were on duty on all these occasions.

In the same year, widespread interest was aroused in the tracking ability of the Force's Alsation dog Rennie which, in 1958, had been purchased from and trained with its policeman handler at the Metropolitan Police Dog Training Establishment, Keston, Kent.

Rennie's most important case is an interesting one. About ten o'clock one evening in March, it was learned that a house in Argyll Crescent, occupied by an elderly widow, had been broken into. Detectives, the dog-handler and Rennie were sent there. About the same time, information was received that a house in nearby Burnside Gardens had also been broken into. The dog-handler was told of both crimes, but fortuitously, not the number of the house in Burnside Gardens. As instructed, he went to the lane at the rear of the house in Argyll Crescent and at the back gate, Rennie picked up a scent and followed it along the garden path to a broken ground floor window, then, returning to the gate, the dog followed the scent to the burgled house in Burnside Gardens. Rennie, on a long lead, had actually entered the second house by an open door before the handler caught up with him! It was obvious from the dog's behaviour that the two crimes were connected.

Inside the house in Argyll Crescent, Rennie showed considerable interest in two rugs upon which the intruder(s) had obviously stood. The handler rolled these rugs into acetate sheeting and removed them to his van.

Two brothers were suspected of the crimes. Accordingly, the dog handler and Rennie went with the detectives to the home of one of these brothers on the first floor of a tenement in George Street. The handler laid one of the rugs on the ground floor common passage. Rennie sniffed at the rug, then went upstairs to the first floor, but from the dog's behaviour the handler concluded that several hours had elapsed since the person, who had stood on the rug, had been there. Rennie was then withdrawn. The detectives found that the suspect had left home about six o'clock that night! An hour later the experiment was repeated, but this time the result was quite different. Rennie bounded up the stairs to the suspect's home — he having just returned! He was arrested and taken to police headquarters. His shoes were placed in a polythene bag.

A scent discrimination test was then carried out by a uniformed Inspector, who had nothing whatever to do with the case. He obtained boots and shoes from policemen on duty and placed them along with one of the suspect's shoes on the floor of the police gymnasium. Outside the room Rennie again sniffed at one of the rugs. He was then allowed into the gynmasium without harness, where he sniffed amongst the shoes eventually picking out the suspect's one, which he carried to his handler. The test was repeated with the suspect's other shoe, with the same result.

The dog-handler was then directed to the other brother's home, a semi-detached house in North Anderson Drive. At the gate Rennie was given one of the rugs. He sniffed at it then led his handler to the brother's door, completely ignoring the adjoining house. The brother was then arrested and taken to police headquarters, where similar scent discrimination tests were carried out with his shoes. The same positive results were obtained.

The brothers were tried at the Sheriff Court later that month, found guilty of the crimes and were each sentenced to six months' imprisonment. When the dog-handler gave his evidence, he was accompanied in court by Rennie.

It was not the work of the dog alone which proved the charges against them. Taken into account were other factors: bank notes found in the possession of one brother were identified by the owner; fibres found on a rose bush at the house were identical to fibres from the coat of the other brother; and a footprint of one of them was found at the scene of the crimes.

The same house in Argyll Crescent was broken into in a similar manner about a year later, in January 1960, and again Rennie was involved. The dog picked up a scent in the house which led him to an axe, which apparently had been handled by the intruder, and to rugs in front of a wardrobe and a dressing table, both of which had been ransacked.

One of the same two brothers was suspected and it was known that he had changed his place of abode to one of six flats in a tenement house in Ferrier Gardens. As in the previous case, Rennie was taken to the house and at the entrance was given one of the rugs. He sniffed at it, then led police officers to a top flat, on the door of which was a nameplate which did not bear the suspect's name. However, when a policeman knocked on the door the suspect himself opened it! He was arrested and taken to police headquarters where Rennie identified his shoes, as previously.

When arrested, the suspect had in his possession a torch and a pair of gloves and after his arrest he made some highly significant remarks, which, taken together with Rennie's actions, secured his conviction.

On this occasion an appeal was lodged against the conviction, but it was refused at the High Court of Justiciary in May 1960 'on the grounds that the admissions and explanations of the accused as given in the evidence by the police, taken in conjunction with the evidence given as to the behaviour of the dog, were sufficient to justify a conviction'.

An interesting sequel to the cases occurred on 19 June 1969, when 'The Swinney Trophy' was presented by Dr George Swinney, Lenzie Hospital, Dunbartonshire, to be awarded annually to the best police dog at the Scottish Regional Police Dog Championships. Dr Swinney presented the cup in memory of his parents Baillie and Mrs Swinney. His mother was the widow who had lived in the house in Argyll Crescent at the time of the burglaries.

However, the most serious crime of the year was committed on 21 May. Late that afternoon, two young girls, who had been playing on the Broad Hill, saw a man and a woman sitting together on the grass. Shortly afterwards they saw the man walk away leaving the woman lying there. The children approached and saw that the woman was lying still, her face and head covered with blood. The police arrived and found the woman had been strangled with a shoe lace. An Aberdeen man, twenty-four-year-old labourer John Douglas Leslie, was later arrested and charged with her murder. He was found guilty at the next sitting of the High Court and sentenced to Life Imprisonment.

1960 was the year of 'The Willink Report'. On 25 January, Her Majesty The Queen appointed a Royal Commission to review the constitutional position of the police throughout Great Britain and the arrangements for their control and administration. Sir Henry Willink, BT., M.C., Q.C., was appointed chairman and there were fourteen other members. The Commission were required to consider the constitution and functions of police authorities; the status and accountability of members of police forces, including chief officers of police; the relationship of the police with the public and the means of ensuring that complaints by the public against the police were effectively dealt with; and the broad principles which should govern the remuneration of the Constable, having regard to the nature and extent of police duties and responsibilities and the need to attract and retain an adequate number of recruits with the proper qualifications.

The Commission submitted an *interim* report on 15 November 1960. It dealt entirely with the question of remuneration and recommended that the pay of policemen should be substantially increased. One of the reasons for the recommendation related to a Constable's responsibilities:

'34. The police representatives submitted to us that the Constable is thus unique among the subordinates in the nature and degree of

I

the responsibility he is required to exercise. We accept this. In a country jealous for the liberty of the subject, powers of arrest are not to be lightly conferred or wantonly exercised; and the Constable must be vigilant both to use his authority adequately and instantly as occasion demands, and at the same time never to exceed it. We are satisfied that this individual responsibility is more onerous than any delegated to, or assumed by, a member of any comparable profession or occupation. Responsibility of this kind, to be properly and reasonably exercised, demands high moral standards and a nice exercise of judgement.'

The Commission recommended that Constables should be paid six hundred pounds per annum rising to nine hundred and ten after nine years, with two supplementary payments of thirty pounds a year, after seventeen and twenty-two years' service. These recommendations were approved by the Government, as were corresponding increases for higher ranks.

The Commission's final report dealt with the other terms of reference and the more important conclusions and recommendations were later embodied in new police legislation or regulations.

Towards the end of the year another change in conditions was made. The Town Council rescinded their resolution passed in 1934, that members of the Force above the rank of Constable should, as a general principle, be required to retire on pension on completion of the period of service entitling them to do so, on the grounds that their retention was not in the interest of efficiency. Hereafter, the Chief Constable was to be required to report on each policeman who desired to remain in the Force beyond his pensionable date.

The improved conditions which resulted from 'The Willink Report' had the desired effect on recruitment during 1961 and twenty-one Constables were appointed from three hundred and forty-nine applicants. However, by the end of the year, the Force was still forty-five under strength, a state of affairs occasioned during the year by the raising of the establishment from two hundred and eighty-one to three hundred and twenty-six.

The event of 1961, however, was the brutal murder of a six-year-old girl at Woodside on 8 January. The investigations strained the resources of the Force to the limit and those of the Criminal Investigation Department in particular. The Special Constabulary were called upon to aid the regular Force in patrol duties.

The murder hunt was widespread. Practically every police force in the United Kingdom was involved in tracing and interviewing people who had been in the city at the time the crime was committed. However, despite this extensive effort, the crime remained undetected at the end of the year and remained so until November 1963, when the perpetrator was eventually arrested, but regretfully not before he had claimed another victim.

Of a kind and understanding disposition, Chief Constable Matheson was deeply conscious of the anguish and suffering being experienced by the girl's relatives during the prolonged enquiry and it was regrettable that he died before the murderer was eventually brought to justice.

When the Chief Constable died on 14 March 1963, at the early age of fifty-eight, the Town Council minuted a glowing tribute to his memory, part of which reads:

'Mr. Matheson had a wide experience of police work and he brought to the performance of his duties a wealth of knowledge, a sound judgement, a deep understanding of human nature and a full measure of Christian charity, derived from the high principles on which, as a devout Churchman, he guided his life.'

Chief Constable Matheson's term of office was one of consolidation rather than experimentation. He was committed to the 'Team System of Policing', and apart from a slight modification — the creation of a Centre District policed by foot patrols — the system functioned more or less as originally conceived. He was, however, acutely aware that the manpower situation left much to be desired and over the years he was relatively successful in building up the strength of the Force to a more realistic level. He also took steps to ensure the good deployment of his men throughout an expanding city by arranging the provision of several new sub-stations: Diamond Street in 1957; Byron Square and Brierfield Terrace in 1958; Bridge of Dee in 1959; and Mastrick in 1963. His period in office also saw the retiral, in October, 1961, of the Commandant of the Special Constabulary, Dr. Albert D. Imper, M.B.E., and the appointment to the post of the present Commandant Mr. William H. Stephen, White Lodge, Milltimber.

Matheson was ably assisted in his work by the two officers who, in turn, held the appointment of Deputy Chief Constable — Chief Superintendent Robert Petrie McKerron till 1960, and thereafter Chief Superintendent Hugh Rose MacQueen, each of whom, in his own way, contributed much to the efficiency of the Force during their service. Indeed, on Matheson's death, it fell to MacQueen to guide the destinies of the Force until a successor was appointed.

Chapter Fourteen

1963-70

MacQueen's six months' spell of command was an eventful one. On 31 May 1963, in a house in Jackson Terrace, twenty-one-year-old labourer Henry John Burnett shot and killed the merchant-seaman husband of the woman with whom he had been consorting. Armed with the gun, he then robbed a man of his car and fled the city but was arrested soon afterwards near Ellon by officers of the Scottish North-Eastern Counties Constabulary. He stood trial at the High Court of Justiciary in July, was found guilty of 'Capital Murder' and sentenced to death. The sentence was carried out at Craiginches Prison, on 15 August. Supporters of the movement for the abolition of the death penalty demonstrated outside the prison on the morning of the execution, but there was no reprieve and the judicial hanging — the last in Aberdeen — was carried out in accordance with the law. Capital punishment was abolished two years later. Initially, the abolition of the death penalty for murder was for a period of five years, but in 1970, Members of Parliament, on a free vote, decided against its re-introduction.

On 7 July, the search began for a seven-year-old boy, who had been reported missing from his home in Justice Street. During the evening, he had gone out to look for his brother and had not returned. At the time there was no reason to suspect anything sinister, but in accordance with normal police procedure, extensive enquiries were made in an endeavour to trace the boy. Business premises, allotments and waste ground were searched and parts of Aberdeen Harbour were dredged but without success. A description of the missing child was circulated through the media of press, radio and television and many people supplied information about having seen boys, similar in appearance to the missing child, playing in the Harbour area or on the rocks at the Footdee end of the Beach Esplanade. The fate of the boy, of which more will be written later, was not to be revealed until November, when the solution to the baffling child-murder at Woodside in January 1961, was also provided.

On 29 July 1963, a special meeting of the Town Council was held for the purpose of interviewing four candidates for the post of Chief Constable. Of course, Chief Superintendent MacQueen had been debarred by the Secretary of State for not having the necessary period of service in another police force. Hence the candidates were Chief Superintendent James S. Beattie, Edinburgh City Police; Superintendent Robert Murison, B.L., Lanarkshire Constabulary; Chief Superintendent William McG. Smith, M.A., City of Glasgow Police; and Chief Constable David Williamson, Greenock Burgh Police. The Council selected Chief Superintendent Smith and, with the concurrence of the Secretary of State, he took up the appointment on 1 September 1963, at a salary of two thousand nine hundred and forty pounds.

William McGregor Smith had graduated M.A. at Glasgow University in 1930 and had joined the City of Glasgow Police in 1933. After duty on the beat, in plain clothes, and as an instructor in the Glasgow Police Training School, he was promoted to the rank of Sergeant in 1939 and thereafter through the higher ranks of the Force and at the Scottish Police College, to become, in 1961, Chief Superintendent in charge of the Glasgow Northern Division, the position he held at the time of his Aberdeen appointment.

Shortly after the arrival of the new Chief Constable in November, the city made the headlines when the remains of the missing seven-year-old boy referred to earlier, were found in the greenhouse of an allotment on Castlehill. The grim news was accompanied by the brief statement that a man had been arrested in connection with the boy's death and with the death of the six-year-old girl at Woodside three years before!

It was the chance remark of a six-year-old boy during an interview in connection with indecent offences alleged to have been committed against him and other children that sparked off police enquiries at the allotment. The child said that the missing boy, who had been his best friend, had also visited the allotments. Other children told how a man had been in the habit of giving them money and sweets.

This link with the missing boy was reported to a senior police officer and a major enquiry was launched leading to the recovery of the boy's remains beneath the earthen floor of the greenhouse and the arrest of the allotment holder, thirty-nine-year-old labourer James John Oliphant, for his murder. Examination of the boy's remains revealed wounds similar in character to those inflicted on the child victim of the Woodside murder.

When arrested, Oliphant admitted causing the death of both children.

He was subsequently charged with the murders; with assaulting a third child 'by placing a looped rope round his neck and over a hook, pulling on the rope and constricting the child's neck', and with other offences against children. On account of the accused's mental condition, the murder charges were later reduced to culpable homicide and at the High Court of Justiciary on 11 February 1964, Oliphant was ordered to be detained for life in the State Hospital at Carstairs.

From his experience in Glasgow, the new Chief Constable appreciated the value of a Police Underwater Search Team and accordingly, at the beginning of 1964, he formed such a unit in Aberdeen. Seven Constables underwent a course of instruction under the supervision of Royal Navy personnel from H.M.S. *Condor*, Arbroath. On completion of this initial course, one policeman received advanced training at the headquarters of the diving specialists, who supplied the major part of the Unit's equipment. During the course of its first year, the Unit proved its worth and carried out diving operations in the Rivers Dee and Don and in the Harbour.

The typhoid fever epidemic of 1964 attracted much undesirable publicity to the city. However, the standard of hygiene achieved by the citizens and the good-natured manner in which they observed the restrictions imposed to limit the spread of the disease, brought much favourable comment. Hundreds of people were affected, including two members of the Force.

On Saturday, 27 June 1964, towards the end of the outbreak, Her Majesty The Queen paid an official visit to the city, calling on the Lord Provost at the Town House and meeting officials closely connected with the epidemic. Her Majesty's visit was made in the late evening, when the reception she received from the public was tumultuous and quite beyond all expectations. Fortunately for the police, the vast crowds co-operated to the full.

Following the outbreak, the Corporation, in conjunction with the Chamber of Commerce and other city interests, launched a 'Bon-Accord Fortnight' from 25 July to 8 August. During this period there were daily events, and as all these attracted large crowds, policing arrangements were extensive.

Chief Constable Smith's second year was not without incident in so far as cases of homicide were concerned. One evening in October, a man was found stabbed to death in a lavatory of a public house in Market Street. His assailant, twenty-two-year-old James Connor Smith, was arrested, charged with murder, convicted and sentenced to Life Imprisonment. Two months later, in a house in East North

Street, after a drinking party, a woman assaulted a man with a broken bottle inflicting injuries on him from which he died. Barbara Torliefson, a woman of thirty-eight, was later convicted of Culpable Homicide and sentenced to imprisonment for seven years. Also in December 1964, sixty-one-year-old Henry Bruce was found dead in his flat in George Street. He had died as a result of head injuries. The motive appeared to be robbery, but no one has yet been brought to trial for this crime.

During 1964, experiments were carried out by a member of the Force to produce miniaturised radio equipment. By December, a prototype receiver — basically a converted pocket transistor radio — was built. Initial tests proved very satisfactory and so successful was a demonstration to the Watching and Lighting Committee, that in January 1965, they allocated one hundred and fifty pounds for another fifteen.

These units were put into service in July 1965 and the benefits soon became evident. The receivers operated on the same frequency as that of the mobile units and therefore policemen carrying these receivers were aware of everything that was going on and indeed, on occasions, were in a more favourable position to give immediate attention to urgent incidents.

It was realised, of course, that two-way communication would be better and manufacturers were contacted and invited to demonstrate personal radio equipment immediately it became available. It was not until February 1966, that the first piece of manufactured equipment was shown.

The Aberdeen Force has progressed through the ages largely because it was led by men of initiative and foresight. In the field of personal radio communications, former Chief Constable William Anderson had remarkable foresight when, in his farewell address to the Force in 1932, he forecast that in years to come policemen patrolling the streets would be able to keep in constant communication with their headquarters by means of personal radios. He visualised radio receivers built into policemen's helmets and indeed, had the helmet been retained, this forecast might well have been correct.

Smith too, was a man of vision. He foresaw that the continued efficiency of the Force depended upon the existence of an intensive training programme, not only for new recruits and the younger members of the Force, but also for men with longer service, who had reached or were reaching, the middle and higher ranks. The 'Higher Training' for this older group was designed to broaden their outlook

and improve their professional knowledge. He intensified local training and sent officers on national courses for criminal investigation,
administration, crime prevention, police driving and other specialised
duties. In the realms of 'Higher Training', he sent Inspectors and
Sergeants on courses of three and six months' duration at the Scottish
Police College and to Business Management Courses at Robert
Gordon's College, Aberdeen. In 1964, when the first year-long
Accelerated Promotion Course was held in Scotland — designed to
expedite the promotion of young men of special ability — he was grati-
fied when a detective Constable in the Force was one of the twelve
selected to attend.

The Chief Constable was acutely aware of the need for good relations between the public and the police. He promoted press liaison,
encouraged visits of organised parties to his headquarters and advised
officers, at all levels, to become interested and involved in the affairs
of the community. In 1965, he assisted Grampian Television Limited
in the production of a five-minute weekly programme entitled
'Police News'. The first edition appeared on 29 June 1965. The programme was conceived as a means of relaying information on crime,
traffic and other police matters. The Aberdeen Force undertook the
collation of material from other police forces covered by the television
company's network and uniformed constables were trained to act as
announcers.

Members of the Royal Family paid three visits to the city during
1965, each of which necessitated the usual police attention. The visit
of His Royal Highness, The Duke of Edinburgh in October, caused
some sensation — he arrived by helicopter at Summerhill School!

The year ended on a sad note, with the death on 25 October, of the
Deputy Chief Constable Hugh Rose MacQueen, M.B.E. The feelings
of all who knew this popular officer were aptly summed up by the
Chief Constable in these words: 'Mr. MacQueen was an excellent
Police Officer and a most energetic personality. He was well known
throughout the City and his loss is personal to all ranks in the Force.'

During 1966, the whole system of communication was reviewed
and modernisation begun. Following the successful experiments with
pocket radio receivers in 1965, a number of personal radio sets were
purchased. At the same time, the Town Council approved the replacement of the existing telephone system with the most modern of its
kind. The opportunity was also taken to eliminate duplication of
facilities and to discard the old system of pillars and kiosks, which had
given valuable service but had become redundant.

The greater volume and complexity of communication required a more efficient system of control. Consequently a properly equipped Information Room was brought into operation simultaneously with the new switchboard and two-way personal radios. The new Information Room was controlled by a Sergeant, assisted by civilian assistant controllers.

By 1966, the strength of the Force had been raised to three hundred and sixty-eight policemen and one hundred auxiliaries: sixty-six civilians, twenty-four Traffic Wardens and ten cadets. The Wardens took over the duty of enforcing local parking legislation in the central area of the city on 19 April.

The 1966 inspection of the Aberdeen Force was carried out by Andrew Meldrum, Esq., c.b.e., who in 1965, had taken over duty as H.M. Inspector from Thomas Renfrew, Esq., c.b.e., b.l. During his earlier police career, Meldrum had been, in turn, Chief Constable of Inverness, of Angus and of Fife. In 1966 he was appointed to a new post of Her Majesty's Chief Inspector of Constabulary, with the ex-Chief Constable of Angus, John James Dingwall, o.b.e., becoming H.M. Inspector.

During 1967, the Chief Constable continued his policy of promoting closer contact with the community by setting up a Youth Liaison Section. It comprised a Sergeant and a Constable who directed the activities of selected Beat Constables who were required, as part of their duties, to deliver a series of prepared talks on police work to school children and to youth and community organisations. Within two years, more than thirty policemen were giving the talks and it soon became evident that the object was being achieved — an improved personal relationship between the police and the young people concerned.

Another feature of community involvement followed in June 1970, when the Town Council consented to policemen enrolling as members of the crew of the Aberdeen Inshore Rescue Boat, which is affiliated to the Royal National Lifeboat Institution. It was recognised that police participation in this venture would improve the efficiency of the Inshore Rescue Service. Selected officers — all volunteers — were thereafter trained by a member of the Royal National Lifeboat Institution and made available for call-out in emergencies.

The training of the youngest members of the Force, the Cadets, was also scrutinised and improved by Smith. In addition to departmental training, facilities were provided for Day-Release courses at the Aberdeen College of Commerce and for 'Adventure Training' courses at establishments in the North of Scotland. His interest in Cadet training culminated in the holding of the first Scottish Police Residential Cadet Course at Johnston Hall, University of Aberdeen, from 13 August till 5 September 1968, with the Chief Constable as Commandant. Ninety-six Cadets from forces throughout Scotland attended. The course was designed to engender team spirit and to foster a common consciousness and pride in the Police Cadet Service. The syllabus was arranged in discussion with the Department of Extra-Mural Studies at Aberdeen University.

The introduction of a Scottish Higher National Certificate in Police Studies in 1968 interested many members of the Force and to this end, three Constables along with six officers from other Scottish Forces attended short Block Release Courses over a period of two years at Aberdeen College of Commerce, under the auspices of the Scottish Council for Commercial, Administrative and Professional Education. During the next two years, education for police officers was taken a step further when four members of the Force embarked upon full-time degree courses at the University of Aberdeen, two to study for their LL.B. and two for their M.A.

An event which made the news towards the end of 1969 was a Rugby Football Match held at Linksfield Park between a North of Scotland Select and a South African Touring Team. The games throughout the tour had been occasions for demonstrations by opponents of the South African Government's racial segregation policy of 'Apartheid', and the Aberdeen game was no exception. Three hundred and sixty policemen were required to be on duty inside and outside the ground to control the demonstrators. One hundred and ninety-four Aberdeen policemen were on duty; the remainder came from the forces of Angus, Dundee and Scottish North-Eastern Counties. In the light of conduct experienced at other grounds, special arrangements were made to ensure that both demonstrators and spectators were allowed to exercise their right to go about their lawful occasions. Although ninety-eight persons were arrested during the match, the conduct of the police officers concerned was the subject of much favourable comment. A feature of the occasion, which made the news, was the employment of several policemen, dressed in police shirts and trousers and wearing football boots, to chase and detain demonstrators who had encroached upon the field of play.

A milestone in the Force's history was reached on 7 May 1969, when work began on the building of a new headquarters. The decision to build had been taken by the Town Council in 1964 and thereafter there had been much discussion as to where it should be located. The site of the existing headquarters plus a few adjoining buildings including the old Aberdeenshire Constabulary headquarters vacated in 1963 was the first to be considered. To build there meant the acquisition and demolition of several old buildings, and the building of the new headquarters in two phases, so that the existing headquarters could be kept fully operational during the period of building. Two other sites were considered. One was an open site on the western fringe of the city, the other was in a more central redevelopment area.

The existing site was adopted. It had several advantages. It formed part of a central complex comprising the existing Sheriff Court and Town House, and the recently built Municipal office block; and it had convenient access to main distributor roads.

To Aberdeen's City Architect — George McI. Keith, A.R.I.B.A., A.M.T.P.I., and his successor Thomas C. Watson, A.R.I.B.A., A.R.I.A.S. — fell the task of designing the building and carrying the project through to completion. A Chief Inspector was appointed liaison officer. Detailed consideration was given to the future requirements of the Force. Indeed, it was planned at first to include a heliport on the roof. This feature was later abandoned following advice from the Minister of Civil Aviation who considered that the number of high buildings in the vicinity might create a hazard for landing and take-off.

As it happened the first phase was to consist of a seven-storey main block; two-storey traffic department wing, with link to main block at north-east corner of site; two-storey uniform department wing, with link to main block at south end of site, and two-storey cell block between the existing headquarters and the Sheriff Court building — to be completed by May 1972. The second phase was to involve extending the uniform department wing to link with the cell block, police court and assembly hall gymnasium complex — to be completed by 1974.

By comparison with the new building project, the other developments in the Force seemed insignificant. Yet they were highly important from the point of view of efficiency. The system of policing had been altered to take account of the changing character of the city and to introduce the best elements of Unit Beat Policing as recommended by the Home Office Police Research and Planning Department. 'Panda' vehicles were introduced in October 1968. These provided mobility for the foot patrol officers working from substations on the periphery of the city. The existing mobile patrols were required to police a determined 'Inner Zone', and beat officers were deployed in the centre of the city. To meet these requirements a further three sub-stations were erected: Hazlehead in 1965, Cairncry in 1967 and Tillydrone in 1970.

In October 1969, a gift was received by the Force which established 'The Chief Constable's Award'. This award may be made in January of each year, at the sole discretion of the Chief Constable, to the member of the Force, who has rendered the most outstanding service to the Force or Community during the preceding year.

Six months later, the Town Council received notification from the Secretary of State that he intended to submit to Her Majesty The Queen the name of Mr William M. Smith, M.A., The Chief Constable, for the post of H.M. Inspector of Constabulary for Scotland in succession to Mr John Dingwall who had retired. The Town Council agreed to the proposal and unanimously concurred with the remarks of the Convener of the Watching and Lighting Committee, Councillor Norman Hogg, who, in paying tribute to the Chief Constable for the services rendered by him during his seven years in office, referred to the efficient and helpful manner in which he had always discharged his duties and to the honour conferred upon him by the appointment, an honour in which the City shared. A further honour was bestowed on the Chief Constable two months later when he was awarded the O.B.E. in The Queen's Birthday Honours List.

Chapter Fifteen

1970-72

When Chief Constable Smith became Her Majesty's Inspector of Constabulary for Scotland on 1 July 1970, command of the Force passed to Assistant Chief Constable John Nicol, a Perth man who had joined as a Constable in 1935 and by 1965 had risen to become Deputy Chief Constable. Two years later, following a revision in the rank structure, Chief Superintendent Nicol as he then was, became the city's first Assistant Chief Constable. He was awarded the M.B.E. in 1970.

Nicol was deeply involved in the new headquarters project and determined that it would become one of the finest in the country. Members of the City's Watching and Lighting Committee, in particular its Convener, Councillor Norman Hogg, C.B.E., J.P., LL.D., became deeply interested in the project which proceeded according to plan.

Like MacQueen before him, Nicol was not eligible for the appointment of Chief Constable and the post was advertised at a salary of four thousand two hundred and seventy pounds. On 27 August 1970, from a short leet of eight candidates, Mr Alexander Morrison, Assistant Chief Constable of Staffordshire County and Stoke-on-Trent Constabulary was selected. The other candidates were Chief Superintendents and Superintendents from Scottish Police Forces.

Mr Morrison, a native of Lewis in the Outer Hebrides, began his police career in 1948, as a Constable in the Metropolitan Police serving in the east-end of London. He achieved rapid promotion and in 1963, at the age of thirty-six, was the youngest senior police officer ever to attend the Senior Command Course at the English Police College, Bramshill, Hampshire. In 1968 he was appointed an Assistant Chief Constable of Staffordshire County and Stoke-on-Trent Constabulary, from which post he took up the Aberdeen appointment on 1 November 1970. At forty-three years of age, he became the youngest serving Chief Constable in Scotland.

Morrison took charge of a force of three hundred and sixty-nine policemen and one hundred and seventeen civilians. The revised rank structure previously referred to, provided for one Chief Constable, one Assistant Chief Constable, one Chief Superintendent, four Superintendents, five Chief Inspectors, twenty Inspectors, forty-eight Sergeants and two hundred and eighty-nine Constables. Earlier in the year, an application had been made to increase the establishment by a further thirty-six, to offset the effect of the introduction of a forty-hour working week for policemen, but the Government of the day, in the interests of economy, rejected the proposal.

Morrison soon realised that he was coming to a city not without its share of serious crime. Two weeks before he took up office, a brutal double murder occurred in which the victims were two young married women. Both had been stabbed to death during the afternoon of Monday, 19 October, one in her home in Raeden Crescent, the other in Moir Crescent. The husband of the second victim, thirty-eight-year-old Alexander Stewart, was arrested and charged with both crimes. Stewart had been released from H.M. Prison, Peterhead, on 15 October 1970, and on his return to the city found his wife had been living with another man. Four days later, he visited the other man's wife in her home in Raeden Crescent, and, after an argument, stabbed her to death. He then went to her husband's butcher's shop in Moir Crescent, confronted his wife there and killed her in a like manner. On 26 January 1971, Stewart appeared before the High Court. The presiding judge Lord Cameron, after hearing testimony regarding Stewart's mental condition, concluded he was insane and could not be tried on the indictment. Consequently, he committed Stewart to the State Hospital at Carstairs 'without limit of time'. Ironically, Stewart joined there his younger brother Frank, who had been committed to the hospital in March 1970, for the culpable homicide of an elderly watchman at Persley Quarry, Bucksburn.

The 1970 Annual Inspection of the Force was carried out on 30 December, by Mr David Gray, O.B.E., Q.P.M., H.M. Chief Inspector of Constabulary, who had been appointed Chief of the Inspectorate in 1969, on the retiral of Mr Andrew Meldrum. Previously, Gray had been Chief Constable of Stirling and Clackmannan Constabulary.

On 16 February 1971, the Government issued a White Paper on local government reform, based upon the report published in 1969 of The Royal Commission on the Reorganisation of Local Government in Scotland, which had been set up under the chairmanship of Lord Wheatley, three years before.

The proposals recommended in 'The Wheatley Report' will mean, in effect, the replacement of the existing four hundred and thirty local authorities in Scotland by eight regional authorities and two all-purpose authorities for Orkney and Shetland. The City of Aberdeen and the counties of Aberdeen, Kincardine, and most of Morayshire and Banffshire are to form one region known as the north-east, which is to be divided into five district authorities: Aberdeen, Kincardine — Deeside, Donside, Banff — Buchan, and Moray.

The responsibility for the provision of all major public services including the police falls to regional authorities. The Aberdeen City Police Force will be merged with the Force now known as the Scottish North-Eastern Counties Constabulary and be responsible for policing the north-east region. Nairnshire, that part of Morayshire including the Cromdale district and Grantown-on-Spey, and the Kirkmichael division of Banffshire, presently policed by S.N.E.C.C., will, however, form part of the new Highland Region centred on Inverness.

If the Bill to implement the provisions of the White Paper becomes law — and the aim is to introduce it in the 1972–73 Session of Parliament — then, by 1975, Aberdeen City Police in its present form will cease to exist.

Our story has told how the present Force has fared from its humble beginnings in 1818, in the Old Guard House on the south side of Castle Street, to an ultra-modern headquarters in nearby Queen Street, designed and equipped to meet policing needs of the future. Profoundly important changes have taken place over the years in the scope and nature of police work. The criminal fraternity have diversified their methods and activities and Parliament has passed numerous laws against which all sections of society offend from time to time — a pattern of events which can only extend in the future.

The impact on the police service has been great and will be greater in the future. The policeman's work has become highly responsible and arduous. Only men of integrity, initiative and education, equipped with the best that science and technology can offer, are equal to the task. The inhabitants of the North-East are indeed fortunate, for the existing police forces have always been highly selective in their recruitment and the respective police authorities have, in recent years, provided many of the new buildings and much of the equipment which will be required in the years ahead.

To shape the whole future is not our problem; but only to shape faithfully a small part of it, according to rules laid down. Carlyle

APPENDICES

APPENDIX I
FOCAL POINTS OF EARLY JUSTICE

Heading Hill, the hill immediately east of and at one time adjoining Castlehill, is understood to have been used frequently in early times as a place of decapitation. In all probability it was used as such for the last time in 1615, when Francis Hay was beheaded for the murder of Adam Gordon. The hill was also the scene of many roastings, when a number of witches were cremated between 1590 and 1632. The punishment of death by burning was not inflicted after 1740.

The Gallow Hill which overlooks Pittodrie Park, the home of Aberdeen Football Club, was a place of public execution by hanging prior to 1776. The origin of its name needs no explanation and it is significant that it was in close proximity to the Lepers' Croft, which was then located on or about the present-day Advocates Park. The restrictions imposed on lepers were extremely harsh and infringements of their regulations often meant the imposition of the death penalty. The gibbet on the Gallow Hill was used for the last time on 6 November 1776, when Alexander Morrison was hanged for murdering his wife with an axe.

The Quay-head (Weigh-house Square) was for many years another of the city's seats of punishment. There, swearers, adulterers and other unchaste persons were punished by immersion in the dock. Some even suffered death by drowning. The instrument in use was a type of ducking-stool known latterly as 'the cran'. An example of a sentence involving this dreaded tool was recorded in the *Aberdeen Observer* of 4 October 1638. It told how on 1 July 1638, a frail female was sentenced by the Kirk Session 'to be cartit from the mercat croce to the Kay-heid, thair to be dowked at the cran, and thairefter to be put in the correction hous, quhaire shoe shall remain till Witsunday nixt (July 1638 to May 1639) and to be quhipped everie Monday during that space'.

The Correction House referred to stood in the neighbourhood of Correction Wynd to which it eventually gave its name. It was the brainchild of Provost Alexander Jaffray, who took office in 1635. The institution, which was built in 1636, was one of the first of its kind in Scotland and more than fulfilled expectations. To it were sent 'all vagabonds, strong and sturdie beggares, idle and maisterless personyes, strong in bodie and habill to work, servants disobedient to maistris, children disobedient to parentis, leud leivars, pyikers, common scolds and incorrigible harlottis not amending to the discipline of the Kirk'. Inmates of the Institution were gainfully employed in the manufacture of 'broad cloths, kerseys, seys and other coarse cloths'.

Hangman's Brae, later known as Castle Brae, was absorbed into Castle Terrace in 1864. It is understood to have got its name from the fact that the public hangman's house was situated near to present-day Virginia Street and access to it from Castle Street was gained by way of Hangman's Brae and Hangman's Brig', which spanned the canal which flowed there at that time. The post of public hangman was abolished in 1834. The last holder of the office was John Milne, who is believed to have accepted the post in 1805 as an alternative to seven years' transportation for the theft of beehives.

APPENDIX II
(Extract from) City of Aberdeen Rules and Regulations to be Observed by THE TOWN-SERGEANTS. Enacted by the Magistrates and Council, 6 March 1865.

3d, That the Town-Sergeants are to be in attendance at the Town-house from a quarter before Ten, A.M., till Eight o'clock, P.M., or until the Offices in the Town-house shall be shut, unless when at their meals, as after-mentioned, in order to be ready to discharge any duty required of them by any of the Magistrates, Town-Clerk, Town Clerk Depute, Chamberlain, or Procurator-Fiscal, and for which no charge is to be made or allowed, nor for the conveying of Criminals from the Town-house to or from the Prisons. That each Officer shall be allowed two hours daily for his meals, but only two of them shall leave the Town-house at one time for this purpose.

9th, The Town-Sergeants shall act as Police Officers in looking after and detecting criminals, for which no charge shall be made against the Town's funds, farther than the sum already allocated, or to be in future allocated, by the Council.

APPENDIX III
The names of the Provest Baillies and justices of peace
George Cullen, John Jaffray, Mr Alexander Skene, Patrik Moir, William Gray.
Followes the instructiones to be givin be the saids magistrats and justices of peace to the constables to be nominat be them which are relativ not onlie to the aforsaid particulars but also for informeing the saids constables in acting evriething that is to be committit to them be the magistrats of the burghe.

Orders and Instructiones for Constables 1657.

Efter the constables ar Laufullie admittit and have give[n] the ordinarie aith they ar to goe about the particular dueties following, viz.:

1. All the saids constables or any of them as they sall be requyrit sall give ther appearance when and wher the said magistrats sall appoint for giveing informatioun of any breaches of the peace and other misdemeanors and receaveing ordors and derections as the saids magistrats sall injoine and set doune.

2. Ewerie constable in thir respective divisiones sall apprehend all suspitious persones who ar night walkers and canot give ane good accompt of themselves and bring them to the magistrats to be taikin ordor with as accords. As lykways all wagabunds, idle sturdie beggars and egiptianes. As lykways all idle persones who have no means to live upoun and will not betack themselves some traid.

3. All constables sall apprehend any guiltie of slauchter murther thift or any other capitall cryme and sall requyr the assistance of his nichtbours and bring them to the magistrats.

4. They sall requyr the assistance of the nichtbours for setling of any frey or stir betuixt parties and if any partie sall flie to ane hous the constable sall follow to the hous and if the dores be shut he sall requyr the master or keeper to mack oppin dores which if they refuis he sall tack witnes therupon and the constabl may follow in ane fresh persuit albeit the partie flie without the bounds of his charg. And he sall desyr concurrence.

5. They ar to tack up ane exact roll of all the persones inhabitants within ther precincts maill and femall abov ten yeirs of aige.

6. They ar to requyr all new incummers to present ther testimonialls to ane of the magistrats that ane not of the samen may be taikin in the register for testimonialls. And they sal delat all such as have not testimonialls. And thos that sall set houss to such without aquanting the magistrats or sall fie any servants wanting testimonialls.

7. They ar to mark and delat all unfrie brewars within ther precincts.

8. They ar to delat all persones that ar fund tacking the name of god in waine or any other ways swearing or cursing especiallie in the opin streits and upon mercat dayes as lykways all pykers and any under ane ill report of ther nichtbour for any scandall or miscariage.

9. They sall delat all fornicators and whormongers that come to their knowledge.

10. They sall delat all drunkards and such as haunt taverns or ail houss efter nyne acclock at nicht and such as sell drink in forbiddin tyms or till men be drunk in ther houss or such as sell drink at ane higher rait then is containt in the touns statuts.

K*

11.   They sall delate all saboth breakers and such as wait upon the publick ordinances of gods worship or bracks the Lords day any other maner of way. And for this end constables ar to goe thorow the toune in tyme of ser["]mon and also efter sermons tuo or thrie of them (per vias) to observe what ordor is keepit in the toun upone the Lords day.

12.   They sall delate all scolds and tulyears and such as mack pleys.

13.   They sall delate children come to yeirs of discretione that ar disobedient to parents and servants that ar unrulie and disobedient to ther masters as also such servants as sall be fund to be steallers or pykers of ther masters goods or househel[d] provisioun.

14.   They sall delat such as ar transgressors of any of the statuts publishit be the magistrats that they may be punishit accordinglie.

15.   They shall have four generall meettings the begining of each quarter for considering all things past in the preceeding quarter and other things relating to their severall charges.

16.   They shall meett each munday at nyne acloak in the morning in the laigh councill house for keeping their weekly courts and ilk absent to be fyned in twelfe shilling Scots toties quoties and any constable that shall be found negligent of his duty to be censured as the magistrats shall think fitt.

APPENDIX IV

INSTRUCTIONS from the Magisrates of Aberdeen to Charles Clapperton, appointed Town Keeper and one of the Constables of the said City and Liberties 24 April 1783.

1.   You are hereby authorised to apprehend all sturdy Beggars and all Disorderly or Suspected Persons found within the Town who can give no account of themselves and follow no Trade or Employment or who have no visible means for Support of themselves or their Families, and when apprehended to bring them before some of the Magistrates for Examination.

2.   You are to endeavour to procure Information of all Beggars or other poor persons of whatsoever Sort who may come into the Town from the Country and of the houses where they resort to or reside and immediately upon getting such Information you are to give in the same to some of the Magistrates in Writing along with a List of the Strangers and Landlords Names.

3.   You are likewise to Endeavour to get Information of all such persons as haunt and Entertain in their Houses dissolute, abandoned and debauched Company, and inform the Magistrates thereof as well as of the Names of the Persons who keep and frequent such Houses as also

all such Persons who may be guilty of or concerned in Riots or any kind of Mischief on the Public Streets either by Night or day.

4. You are daily to perambulate the Public Streets and take notice That the Whole of them be cleaned and the dung removed therefrom by the Scavengers against the hours appointed for that purpose and you are likewise to take Notice of any of the Inhabitants that all be guilty of throwing Water or Nastiness of any kind from their Doors or Windows or of laying down the same upon the high streets at any other times than those directed by the Regulations established by the Council (a Printed Copy whereof is herewith delivered for your Information) and you are immediately to Inform some of the Magistrates of the Transgressors of any of those Regulations so as the Fines thereby Established may be exacted from them.

5. You are particularly to observe if any Person shall be guilty of Injuring or Hurting any part of the Public Works or Buildings belonging to The Town such as The Windows of the Churches, the Public Lamps and Wells, the Canal, Bridges, and Planting on the Denburn etc. and you are immediately upon discovery of such Delinquents to give in the List of their Names to some of the Magistrates in order that they be punished according to their Demerit.

6. That you may be more effectively enabled to Execute your Duty you are hereby Impowered to call for the assistance of any other of the Constables of the Burgh as well as of the Town Officers who are all hereby required to concur with and assist you when necessary as they will be answerable and you are likewise hereby required to give the same assistance and support to any of them when they desire it.

7. As the Magistrates have agreed to give you a suitable and adequate allowance for the Employment of you whole-time in their Service you are therefore not to Engage or be concerned in any other Work or Occupation nor are you to Leave the Town at any time without first acquainting and procuring Liberty for that purpose from some of the Magistrates.

And lastly you are to receive and execute all such further Instructions and Injunctions as any of the Magistrates shall think necessary and expedient to deliver you from time to time.

W. YOUNG, Provost and J.P.
John AULD, Baillie and J.P.
George ADAM, Baillie and J.P.
James PAULL, Baillie and J.P.
Andrew BURNETT, Baillie

APPENDIX V

Regulations for THE DAY PATROLE of the City of Aberdeen.

I.   He is to consider himself engaged for six months, from the time of his admission to a district, while he gives satisfaction; and when he intends to resign, he shall give one month's previous notice to the Sergeant of Police. During the time he remains in the service, he is bound to attend to the provisions of the Police Act, and to observe and obey the following Regulations and Orders, or such others as from time to time may be given him by the Board, or Serjeant of Police.

II.   He must be extremely attentive to sobriety and temperance in his behaviour; active and diligent in the discharge of his duty; and maintain, on all occasions, a calm, civil, and obliging, but firm and steady conduct; not suffering himself to be biassed in the execution of his duty.

III.   He must carry about with him a book, for his own particular transactions, and every thing else that may occur worthy of observation; from which he will make a report to the Serjeant, to be entered in a book kept by him for that purpose.

IV.   He shall exert his utmost activity in searching for, detecting, and apprehending, all persons charged with having committed street robberies, house-breakings, assaults, thefts, pocket-picking, swindling, breaches of the peace, breaking the public lamps, or other crimes or offences, contrary to Law.

V.   He shall apprehend all vagrants and common beggars, when found begging or prowling about, within the bounds of police; and all ballad-singers, or others, causing a crowd of idle people to collect on the streets.

VI.   He shall at all times keep a very watchful and strict eye over persons of the foregoing description; endeavour to learn their haunts; what public-houses and other houses they frequent, and the characters with whom they associate — that he may know them again, and that, when any depredation is committed, the offender may be the more easily traced and discovered.

VII.   He shall narrowly observe the conduct of persons known or suspected of resetting stolen goods: of persons known or suspected of counterfeiting or issuing base money; and of persons keeping disorderly houses, or houses of ill fame; and endeavour to find out by what suspicious persons these houses are frequented.

VIII.   He shall be active in assisting to suppress mobs and riots, and in apprehending those concerned therein.

IX.   When a strayed child is found on the street, he shall take charge of such child; and if its residence be not known, he shall conduct it to the Watch-house.

X. He shall apprehend every person wilfully exposing to view, in any street, road, high-way, or public place, any obscene print, picture, or other indecent exhibition.

XI. He shall apprehend any person wilfully, openly, lewdly, and obscenely exhibiting his or her person, in any street, road, or public highway, or in the view thereof, or in any place of public resort.

XII. He shall apprehend every person wandering abroad, and endeavouring, by the exposure of wounds or deformities, to obtain or gather alms.

XIII. He shall apprehend every person going about as a gatherer or collector of alms, or endeavouring to procure charitable contributions of any nature or kind, under any false or fraudulent pretence.

XIV. He shall observe that no horses are standing or ridden upon the pavements or footpaths; that no barrows or other carriages are left or wheeled thereon; no barrels rolled on them, excepting directly across, on necessary occasions; no sedan chairs, large boxes, bakers' baskets, chimney-sweepers' ladders or bags, water-stands, pails, or buckets, or any other thing, to the annoyance of passengers, be carried or set down on the foot-pavements or paths; or fish, clothes, or other articles, hung upon the front of any house; and that no carpets are dusted over any door or window. He shall also prevent the calling of auctions at the doors of houses or shops; and any person from exposing fruit, or any other article, for sale on any of the streets, excepting Castle Street or Green.

XV. That no coach, chaise, cart, or other carriage, nor riders on horseback, do pass through the streets, in a furious manner; and that no chaise-driver sit in his chaise while driving.

XVI. That all carters keep by their horses, and have the bridle, halter, or reins, in their hand; and that they be on the near side of their horses; and that they do not walk on the foot-pavement or footpath, while driving.

XVII. That no carter ride on his cart, unless the horse be harnessed with double reins.

XVIII. That all carts and other carriages be drawn, as much as possible, in one line, so as that a free passage may be kept in the streets.

XIX. He shall not allow coal carts to be backed towards the foot-pavement, but must see that they are drawn up alongside the cirb stone. Nor shall any other carts be permitted to do so, except for purposes absolutely necessary in conducting business.

XX.   That all waggons and carts have the owner's name, residence, and number, placed on some conspicuous part thereof; and that carts in general be not overloaded, nor the horses therein cruelly treated.

XXI.   That no cart or other carriage be left on the streets unyoked; and that none be left yoked, without some person having charge of the same.

XXII.   That no mason or builder do lay down materials upon the streets, for building, repairs, or alterations without having the authority of the Commissioners or other constituted authority, and giving eight days' previous notice to the Clerk of Police of his intention to do so.

XXIII.   That when any building materials or rubbish are laid down on the streets or footpaths, under the above authority, a lamp or lamps be kept burning at the place, from sun-setting till sun-rising; and when holes or other obstructions are made therein, the same, besides being lighted, must be sufficiently fenced in — all under the orders and to the satisfaction of the Inspector of Police.

XXIV.   That no flower-pots, or boxes for holding plants, be placed on the outside of the window, fronting any street or thorough-fare, unless properly railed in.

XXV.   That no carter of dung, mud, or any sort of rubbish, do over-load his cart, so that it falls off and dirties the streets; and that no whale blubber be driven through the town after eight o'clock morning.

XXVI.   He shall observe that no swine or poultry are permitted to straggle through the bounds of police; and that no snow-balls or squibs are thrown; nor foot-ball, shinty, or other game played; nor any kite or fire-balloon set off; nor slides made, in any of the streets, squares, lanes, or passages.

XXVII.   That no improper or indecent words be written on the walls or doors; that the names of streets, squares, closes, and courts, and the numbers of houses, shops, &c. be not defaced, nor put on in-correctly; and that this be more particularly attended to with respect to shops, immediately after terms.

XXVIII.   That all idle persons, porters, and others, do not stand in crowds, on any of the pavements, footpaths, closes, or passages, to the interruption of passengers.

XXIX.   That the gratings of the sewers be kept clear of any rubbish that may obstruct the water, and that such rubbish be cleared away by the scavenger.

XXX.   He shall not keep a public-house, or sell liquor of any kind, by his wife, or otherwise; or deal in second-hand goods, of any description. He shall not drink any intoxicating liquor while on his station, nor go into a public-house, unless in the necessary execution of his duty; nor shall he ask any new-year's gift from any of the inhabitants.

XXXI. In cases of foul vents, or chimneys taking fire, he shall take such measures as he may think most proper for having the fire extinguished, and afterwards report to the Serjeant. And in the event of any house, &c. taking fire, he shall immediately give notice to the Superintendent of Water Works and Fire Engines, and at the Gas Works, and give assistance in preserving order.

XXXII. That the pavements which are broken and decayed, and the chimney-tops and cans thereon that are in a ruinous or dangerous state, be reported, and that the latter be examined more particularly after a storm. He shall also report if any of the public wells are running to waste, or out of repair, and such houses as are in want of water-spouts. He shall also observe that the regulations for the supply of Water to Shipping are properly attended to, and report all persons contravening them, or those for preventing persons exempted from water assessment, from taking water from any of the wells or water courses under charge of the Commissioners.

XXXIII. That no person commit any breach of any regulations established by the Commissioners, in regard to cleansing the streets, lanes, &c. and removing obstructions therefrom; and particularly, that no dung from private ash-pits, vested in the Board is, carried off, excepting by order of the Inspector.

XXXIV. He may command the assistance of any of the inhabitants, when necessary, in the execution of his duty. He shall bring the offending party directly to the Watch-house, together with the complainer, to substantiate the charge.

XXXV. When he finds himself at a loss how to act, he shall apply to the Serjeant for advice; and he shall take care not to bring himself, or the Board of Commissioners, into unnecessary trouble. He shall in all cases give the inhabitants the most civil answers, and behave with all possible civility to every person; not only to those who have suffered injury, but even to such as are accused of offences.

XXXVI. No swearing or abusive language is, on any account or pretext, to be made use of by those employed as Patrole; nor are they to strike or make use of any offensive weapon, unless such is rendered absolutely necessary in their own personal defence and protection.

XXXVII. That the Officers who act as Patrole shall attend at the arrival and departure of the steam-boats and stage-coaches, in their respective districts, for the purpose of looking after any suspicious characters, besides strictly attending to the carters and porters' regulations, and the provisions of the Police Act, or such other instructions as he may receive from the Board.

XXXVIII.   One half of the Patrole will be allowed to go to church on Sundays and Fast-days, in the forenoon, and the other half in the afternoon; the district of those absent to be inspected by those on duty. But, notwithstanding this, the whole are to patrole the streets, in the morning before sermon, in the interval between sermons, and in the evening after sermon, as on any other day; and to prevent boys and idle disorderly persons from prowling about the streets, assembling in crowds, or behaving or amusing themselves in an improper manner. Also, to prevent the driving of cattle through the town on that day.

XXXIX.   He shall leave the sum of one shilling per week of his wages, in the hands of the Treasurer of Police, as a security for his good behaviour, to be paid him at the end of every six months, if his conduct shall have been unexceptionable; but if he shall be found in the smallest degree contravening or neglecting any of his regulations, these arrears shall not only be declared forfeited, but he shall also be dismissed, at the discretion of the Board.

XL.   He shall, upon his appointment, subscribe and receive a copy of these Regulations and Instructions, and such other additional ones as may be deemed necessary.

XLI.   For the encouragement of the Day Patrole in the discharge of their duty, and to stimulate them the more in discovering and apprehending delinquents, and in the recovery of stolen property, or in finding out the resetters thereof, gratuities will be given them, at the discretion of the Board, according to the activity and ability they have shown in searching for and securing offenders, or where any other service has been performed which appears to the Board to be meritorious, and beyond the ordinary line of duty. But while rewards are thus held out to those Patrolemen who show superior activity, none will be suffered to continue in the service of the Eastablishment who are inactive, or who do not on all occasions show a marked degree of zeal and spirit in the discharge of their duty.

LASTLY.   He must peruse the above Regulations and Instructions, as well as the Police Act, and Bye Laws established by the Board, frequently, so as they may be familiar to him; and he shall always have them in his possession, ready to be shown as his authority for acting, when required.

APPENDIX VI

Roll of Watchmen on duty. 17 & 18th July 1831.

NAMES	STATIONS
William Christie	Patrole.
John Knox	Do.
Alexr. Fraser	Do.
John Gray	West End of Castle Street, Lodge Walk.
Charles Anton	East End of Castle Street, and South End of King Street.
Charles Wilson	Justice Street, Wales Street.
John McHattie	Princes Street, Frederick Street, North End of King Street.
John Paterson	West North Street, Meal-Market Lane.
Innes Pittendrigh	Queen Street, South End of Broad Street.
John Clapperton	East North Street, Shuttle Lane.
Alexr. Rae	North End of Broad Street, and Long-Acre.
John Gray 2th	South End of Gallowgate.
Joseph Massie	North End of Gallowgate.
David Duncan	Causewayend, Hutcheon Street.
George Cowieson	Kingsland Place, Broadford.
Robert Lafferty	North End of George Street, John Street.
William Monro	South End of George Street, Upperkirkgate, Drum's Lane.
James Main	Guestrow, Netherkirkgate, St. Nicholas Street.
George Boyne	Union Street.
John McDonald	Schoolhill, Belmont Street, Backwynd.
Alexr. Burness	Woolmanhill, Spa Street, Black's Buildings.
William Edwards	Green, Carmelite Street, and Carmelite Lane.
George Davidson	Shiprow, Shorebrae.
John Moir	Marischal Street, Quay.
Francis Ruist	James' Street, Quay.
George Smith	Commerce Street, Quay.
Alexr. Watson	Canal Terrace, Catto's Square.
Alexr. Johnston	Waterloo Quay, Links Street.
Alexr. Davidson	Wellington Street, York Street.
Charles McIntosh	Park Street, Constitution Street.
Rodrick McLean	Loch Street, Berry Lane, Young Street.

APPENDIX VII

Roll of Honour. (★ Killed in action or died of wounds. † Accidentally killed during training. ‡ Died from illness contracted on War Service.)

Abel, Robert
Addison, David
Barron, Alexander
Barron, Watson
Bisset, William
Bowie, Peter
Brown, William
Bremner, Alexander★
Cameron, John
Cormack, Andrew
Cormack, James
Coull, Duncan
Coutts, Robert★
Cruickshank, James★
Davidson, George
Davie, Alexander
Douglas, Gordon★
Duncan, George★
Elder, Andrew
Ewen, James
Fordyce, James
Fowlie, Alexander
Fraser, William
Gerrard, George‡
Gibb, Lawrence
Goodall, Robert
Grant, Alexander
Gray, Walter
Grieve, David‡
Groat, George
Grubb, Thomas
Hardie, Frederick
Henderson, Jonathan
Jaffray, John
Jamieson, William
Mackie, James

Mair, Alexander
Mair, John
Middleton, William
Moggach, William
Mortimer, Arthur★
Murdoch, George
Murray, George
Murray, William
Mutch, Charles
M'Donald, Alexander
M'Intosh, James★
M'Kay, John S.
M'Kay, William
M'Leod, William
M'Pherson, Harry
Ogilvie, Alexander
Ogg, Thomas★
Pirie, James†
Robb, Robert
Robertson, Alexander
Robertson, William
Ross, David
Sandison, Hector
Scott, Donald
Sellars, James
Sim, Henry
Slessor, Gordon
Smith, Andrew
Smith, Harry
Taylor, Alexander
Taylor, Duff
Taylor, Francis
Thomson, John
Thom, George
Thow, George
Watt, George

Watt, John
Webster, John
Whyte, Joseph

Wilson, James
Wood, Alexander*
Wood, William

APPENDIX VIII

Police Box system of policing introduced 1929.

SITUATION

1. Baxter Street
2. Victoria Road at South Esplanade West
3. Oscar Road
4. South Crown Street at Crown Street
5. Justice Mills
6. Fonthill Road
7. Holburn Street at Ruthrieston Terrace
8. Anderson Drive at Great Western Road
9. Rubislaw, Queen's Road
10. Queen's Cross, Fountainhall Road
11. Mile-End, Mid Stocket Road
12. Westburn Drive at Cornhill Road
13. Powis Terrace at Clifton Road
14. Great Northern Road, Woodside
15. High Street, Old Aberdeen
16. Bridge of Don
17. Bathing Station
18. York Place
19. King Street at Fire Station
20. Causewayend
21. Loch Street
22. Diamond Street
23. Leadside Road
24. Caroline Place
25. St. Nicholas Street
26. Regent Bridge
27. Dock Street
28. Albert Quay
29. Market Street at Albert Quay
30. Castle Terrace
31. Castle Street
32. Schoolhill
33. Kings Gate
34. Stewart Park
35. Haudagain
36. Sunnyside
37. Hutcheon Street
38. Hazlehead

Index